The
SELF-RESPONSIBILITY
Guidebook

Jessie. I. Dayton

Table of Contents

Chapter 8:   **Natural Nutrition - 99**

-The "ME" Diet
-Diet & Nutrition Guidelines for an Optimal Health:
-Tips on How to Structure Your Diet
-Foods to Reduce and/or Avoid
-Detox & Cleanse!
-The "Detox" Diet Plan
-The Smoothie/Soup/Salad Diet Plan

Appendix

Acknowledgements:

This book was written for, and is dedicated to,
those who need it!

I would like to acknowledge and give a special thank you to
the following:

A. N. / Y. H. / M. H. G. / I. A. / V. H. / N. P. A.

This book would not have been completed without the care
and support of the following individuals:

E. R. J. / H. I. K. / R. G. / L. A. / J. S. / S. S.

S. C. / J. J. / S. J. / K. S. / D. B.

Please use the following email address if you have any
questions pertaining to the contents of this Guidebook:

jessiedayton@hotmail.com

A word to the reader:

-Before you begin reading this Guidebook there are a few things that you need to know. This Self-Responsibility Guidebook is an accumulation of facts and undeniable truths that deal specifically with you and I! It only contains information that I have found through experience to be true and natural in its approach. On the contrary, all other information I have come across that was based only on theory or hypothesis have been excluded. No fads, get-fit-quick schemes, magic pills, or hazardous short-cuts.

-This Guidebook is designed in a presentation-style format to place direct emphasis where it should be, on the facts. It is structured to present the information first and give explanation or analysis only when necessary. This allows us to get right to the truth of the matter that is being presented and discussed.

-Throughout this Guidebook you will come across some words and phrases that are highlighted in bold, italics, or underlined. This is done to place more emphasis on the value and importance of these words and their meanings in relation to your life.

-All numbers and percentages related to the information given within this Guidebook are approximates and may be off by 1 to 2 percent. This in no way changes the value or importance of these numbers as they relate to you.

-Before practicing any form of medicine or trying any diet plan please consult your doctor or health-care professional FIRST!

The sole purpose of this introduction is to provide an explanation as to WHY and HOW this Self-responsibility Guidebook was created...

Introduction

I have always wanted to serve! From a young age I knew that I wanted to provide some sort of service geared toward helping people, I just didn't know what service it would be. These feelings and my curiosity about fitness, nutrition, and wellness led me directly to my first venture as a Certified Personal Trainer. During my first few months I enjoyed helping people increase their level of physical fitness but when it came to serious questions about their nutrition, mental anxiety, or emotional distress, I had very few answers for them. This made me feel incomplete as a Personal Trainer, so I sought ways to further my education by becoming a Certified Integrative Medicine & Nutrition Consultant. The information provided throughout this new certification was amazing and very relevant to my field of study, but I still felt as if there was something lacking that could make me even better.

What I had failed to realize is that it does not matter what new knowledge or information you receive, what matters is do you truly understand it, and more importantly, have you applied the knowledge and information in your own personal life. This 3-fold process of learning (knowledge + understanding + application) allows an individual to gain the necessary **EXPERIENCE** needed so they can in turn share the knowledge they have received with someone else in a proper and responsible manner.

So, the inadequacy I felt earlier was my lack of experience and true understanding of the subjects I was trying to teach as a Personal Trainer. I did not feel right trying to instruct someone when I myself had not practiced what I was trying to preach! Immediately I quit my brief 3-month Personal training practice, I had finally realized that I needed to spend much more time truly understanding and practically applying all of the information and knowledge I had received before I even think about trying to instruct professionally.

At the beginning of my journey my first intent was to serve, not to harm. The field of "Personal Training" covers a wide-range of vital issues that have a direct effect on a person's health and well-being. It is very important that the individual providing the guidance and instruction **KNOWS** the information, **UNDERSTANDS** the fundamental components involved, and has gained the **PERSONAL EXPERIENCE** necessary to teach before attempting to guide anyone, anywhere! Simply stated, I had to fully practice what I wanted to teach, and that is exactly what I did...

For the next 10 years I completely devoted my personal life to truly understanding and practically applying every method, technique, and philosophy I had learned in the areas of fitness, nutrition, and wellness. In the first year of this journey I was fortunate enough to get a job working for the U.S. Army's Morale Welfare and Recreation Program. This organization deals specifically with the fitness, nutrition, and wellness of soldiers and their family members so it was a great opportunity for me to gain much needed experience. Within six months after starting I began teaching a Circuit-training class that I would continually teach, three times a week, for the next 15 years! I did not know at the time, but this class would eventually turn into an 11-week course that covers every aspect of an individual's health and well-being.

The new job and fitness class I was teaching in no way slowed my study, practice, and devotion to mastering every natural method and technique I could find in these fields. In the third year of my self-study I had finally gained the necessary experience to start going more in depth into personal diet, so I added a weekly 30-minute nutritional lecture to my already ongoing circuit–training class and it was a hit! I didn't realize how many people did not know and understand the simple facts involved with weight loss and weight gain. I could now answer those in-depth questions related to personal nutrition, give them the proper instruction and guidelines on how to make healthier decisions, and explain the importance of what they eat and the effect it has on their body.

I was now beginning to feel more complete as a "Personal Trainer", but there was still one more element I needed in my repertoire if I truly wanted to provide the best and most complete service to my clients, and that was the "wellness" component! So directly after adding the nutritional portion to my class I began focusing more of my personal time on the fundamental components of **Integrative Medicine**, especially one of its most popular components - **Mind-body Exercise**. This ancient and natural form of **self-medication** provides guidance on how to maintain mental and emotional well-being by learning how to **train your mind** and **control your emotions**.

For the next 4 ½ years straight I studied the principles of Mind-body Exercise and practiced some of its most popular techniques like Guided Imagery, Breathing Exercises (meditations), and Progressive Muscle Relaxation. This process gave me the experience necessary to finally add the last "wellness" component to my class. In the seventh year of my self-study and career working for the M.W.R. Program I added the final component, a 30-minute session entitled "Meditational Fitness". This short once a week session soon became so popular that I had to add another 30-minute session just to supply the demand for it. Most everyone that tried these new "Meditational Fitness" sessions were astonished at how simple but powerful some of the Mind-body methods and techniques were. I was once again amazed that nearly everyone knew of the "stress response" and its effect on the mind and body, but nearly no one had heard of the "relaxation response", which has an opposing positive effect on the mind and body! The information I provided through these new 30-minute "Meditational Fitness" sessions was actually giving my clients the tools they needed to attain and maintain their mental and emotional well-being!

I finally had it, a class that covered every aspect of an individual's well-being from their **fitness** (how they move), to their **nutrition** (what they consume), to their **wellness** (how they think and feel). I was excited and motivated, my decision seven years earlier that I should gain more experience by first applying this knowledge to myself had truly paid off. I know had the necessary experience to be a responsible and knowledgeable "Trainer".

For the next three years I devoted most of my time restructuring my 1 ½-hour class into an 8-week long Meditational Fitness Program. I wanted to specifically design a course that would provide the necessary information, guidelines, and practical exercises needed so my clients could in time become their own personal trainer, nutritionist, and wellness coach! I knew that in order to do this my new course must have a strong foundation, so I began building it based on the natural and ancient practice of Integrative Medicine. Making this decision made perfect sense, especially since this form of "medicine" is based entirely around helping an individual heal and become more physically, mentally, and emotionally fit.

By the end of my tenth year I finally finished it, my new and exclusive "Meditational Fitness Course". A complete 8-week "Wellness Program" that covered every aspect of an individual's well-being. The only thing I needed now was clients, after working with some of the soldiers in the U.S. Army's "Wounded Warriors Program" I decided that the people who would benefit the most from this new course would be those who had served in a war-time situation and suffered from certain mental and emotional problems like PTSD, Sleep Apnea, and Depression. I needed permission to utilize the soldiers for my new course, so I set up an appointment with their Commander, Head Physician, and Physical Therapists from the local Military Hospital. After giving a 20-minute power-point presentation that explained the course in detail I received the necessary approval to utilize the Wounded Warriors for my program.

To make a long story short, the soldiers loved it! The results from their weekly "Knowledge of Self" survey showed without a doubt that they had improved tremendously in their physical, mental, and emotional fitness. All fifteen of the soldiers that participated in the 3 pilot courses showed an obvious reduction in the symptoms that stemmed from their mental and emotional ailments. The Program was a success! I was given permission by the Commander to continue with the program until half-way through the third course I learned that I would be moving to a different Military base because of down-sizing and base closures. Due to the work I had done for the U.S. Army over the last 11 years I was offered a position as a Fitness Program Manager at a different Installation. This job gave me the authority to create and implement fitness, nutrition, and wellness programs for Soldiers and their family members. For me this was great, I now had the opportunity to expand my Meditational Fitness Course Program and make it available to not just the soldiers but their family members as well.

I knew that if I wanted to make my program available to the entire population it must be provided in a more open format. The best idea I could find was to open an actual Wellness Center, this would allow me the opportunity to offer my Meditational Fitness Course to soldiers and their family members. After receiving permission from my supervisor, I began working immediately to create the first "Wellness Center" or "Spa" within the U.S. Army's Morale Welfare and Recreation Program that was specifically based on Mind-Body Exercise, Natural Nutrition, and Meditational Fitness. The doors opened in July of 2014 and for 3 years straight I had the privilege of providing my Meditational Fitness Course to people from all walks of life with fantastic results.

I still wasn't finished! After celebrating the 1-year anniversary of our Wellness Center I began refining my original 8-week course into a 11-week program. I also realized that I could ensure my clients success even more if they had some type of **study or reading material** that would enable them to continue what they learn in the course at home. So, I began writing, taking everything I had learned over the last 16 years, including the guidelines given in my Meditational Fitness Courses. My goal was to put this information into a written format which was simple to follow and easy to understand. The "Self-Responsibility Guidebook" in your hands right now is the result of this process!

In the pages of this book you will be introduced to a philosophy of complete wellness that covers every aspect of your being. This philosophy is not hard to understand or apply, it is based entirely on natural law and provides an in-depth knowledge of YOU, as a physical, mental, and emotional being.

This Guidebook is specifically designed to help guide you to an optimal level of well-being, it is then your job to maintain it utilizing what you have learned and applied throughout the process. The path to good health starts with YOU, and there is no better time than now to start making the right choices today, that will have a positive effect on your health in the future!

Chapter 1: Knowledge of Self

There is nothing more important than having a knowledge of self!

Every human being should want to know and understand all components of their being so they can in turn know how to utilize themselves to their fullest potential. Our life is defined by how we decide to live, think, and feel with our body, mind, and emotions. These daily decisions we make and the effects that come from them play a major role in determining our overall health and well-being. We have all heard the saying...

"You are what you eat, (body)
You become what you think, (mind), &
You act on how you feel." (emotions)

This saying is not just a fancy play on words it is a **Universal Law** that deals specifically with you and your ability to either shape your own destiny or become your own worst enemy. Each individual is <u>solely</u> responsible for the decisions they make with their body, mind, and emotions. No one decides what you eat, how you think, or how you feel, these decisions are yours alone. The laws that govern these actions cannot be avoided but they can be used to your benefit if you know yourself and understand the power that comes from self-control and self-responsibility...

*"You are what **<u>YOU DECIDE</u>** to eat,*
*you become what **<u>YOU DECIDE</u>** to think, &*
*and you act on how **<u>YOU DECIDE</u>** to feel."*

If we lack knowledge and understanding of these natural laws that govern us we usually end up making harmful and uninformed decisions that become the precursors for pain, disease, or illness in our life. Each decision we make plays a part in shaping our destiny and determining our future health and happiness. This is exactly why knowledge of self and the universal laws that govern our life is of the utmost importance. If you know the law you can use the law to your benefit, instead of becoming a willing victim to it!

Throughout the pages of this Guidebook I have tried my best to provide some of this knowledge and information in its simplest form so you can begin to strengthen yourself by knowing yourself! Once you begin to study and understand the truths and laws that govern your body, mind, and emotions there is no denying the power you have over your own destiny, health, and happiness. Each one of us is an amazing being with tremendous potential and capabilities. Everything we need to manage our health, shape our own destiny, and attain an optimal level of well-being is already within our grasp. It all depends upon your individual level of will-power which includes...

the want to know, the need to understand, and the discipline to apply!

As you begin reading this "Self-responsibility" Guidebook it is a good idea to have a clear understanding of exactly **WHAT** you are (self)responsible for, so let's begin by asking this question...

What are you?

(Take a few seconds to answer this question before you continue)

If the answer you gave to the above question had something to do with your gender, country of birth, profession, or the fact that you are a human being then you are only partially correct. There is also something that you are, and absolutely must be, before you can be anything else or claim any one of the above titles. This "something" that you are is amazing, incredible, and extraordinary! Unfortunately, at the same time it is underappreciated, overlooked, and misused. Despite these attitudes we have toward this amazing "something" it is still what we are! Have you figured it out yet? What are you?

For the last 10 years I have asked this question to my clients and most of them answered by stating their gender, "I am a man" or "I am a woman". Some answered the question by identifying themselves by their culture or country of birth, and even fewer answered by stating their profession or trade, "I am a Soldier", or a "I am a Teacher".

Unfortunately, these answers are only partially correct and disregard a very vital part of what you are. The titles you possess may be important, but they place more emphasis on one single aspect of life as opposed to life itself. The fact that you may be a man, woman, citizen, or a professional is irrelevant if you do not know, understand, and appreciate the "state of being" necessary to claim these titles.

So, let's rephrase the question...

What are you……right now?
(Once again, take a few seconds to answer the question before you continue)

Right! You are ALIVE! That is what you are and obviously must be before you can be anything else! The initial step each individual must take in building a "knowledge of self" is to know and appreciate this amazing fact. Life is a blessing and an opportunity that should be cherished and utilized. Thoughts and feelings of thankfulness and gratitude for life are powerful because they help you produce a positive mind-set which in turn strengthens your mental fitness and ability to combat emotional distress. Every decision or action you make begins first with a thought. This means it is crucial to maintain a positive thought process if you want to produce positive actions and results.

The Learning Process

The next step in building a "knowledge of self" will also help magnify your positivity and appreciation for life. It is a "**learning process**" that involves taking a more in-depth look at the main components of life which include your **body**, **mind**, and **emotions**. The only way to truly understand these vital parts of your being is to **learn** as much as you possibly can about them. The word "learn" is defined in the dictionary as...

*To gain knowledge, understanding, or skill by **study** or **experience**.*

This means that in order to gain knowledge and understanding of your body, mind, and emotions you first have to study them! The more you know and understand all components of your being and how they properly function the more informed and intelligent your decisions and actions will be. Your body is the vehicle, your mind is the control center, and your emotions are the fuel that drive both. Regardless of the role each plays it is still **YOU** that has supreme authority over how they are utilized and are solely responsible for the effects and consequences they produce, whether good or bad. This is exactly why it is so important to build a foundational knowledge of self! You cannot truly maintain an optimal level of physical, mental, and emotional fitness if you do not know and understand each component of your being and the universal laws that govern them.

Throughout the remainder of this chapter I will provide factual information that is directly related to your body, mind, and emotions. It is then your responsibility to study and research this information until you have gained a level of understanding that will enable you to apply this "knowledge of self" in your everyday life. It makes no sense to learn something new, understand its importance and relevance in your life, and then not utilize the information learned for the benefit of self. The process of learning is only complete once you have applied the knowledge learned and gained the experience from it! Experience is vital because it shows you the effects and consequences that come from how you decide to live, think, and feel so you can in turn make better decisions in the future.

The formula for this learning process is simple:

KNOWLEDGE + UNDERSTANDING + APPLICATION = EXPERIENCE (wisdom)

This process is important to know because in order for the following information to be useful in your life it must first be understood and applied. If in this Guidebook you cannot fully understand some of the information provided, then do your own research on these subjects until you fully comprehend them. This requires time and effort which everyone has, regardless of the excuses. Look at how much time is spent on movies, TV series, social networks, video games, and other forms of entertainment on a daily basis. If you simply reduce some of this constant entertainment intake it will provide you with more than enough time to put into the study of self. It is only a matter of time-management and resetting your priorities to include something in your daily practice that helps you understand you!

Chapter 2: Your AMAZING Body!

We are extraordinary! Our body and brain are the most sophisticated and complex machines on this earth by far! The information given below is intended to provide you with a deeper understanding of self and just how intricate, interconnected, and incredible you are!

Extraordinary Facts About Your Body & Brain!

(Your AMAZING Body...)

- Whenever you are seated or standing still your body is still in motion. Right now, the Earth and everything on it is traveling around the sun at around 67,000 miles per hour! Thank goodness for gravity!
- The same star dust generated from exploding stars that consists of hydrogen, nitrogen, carbon, and oxygen atoms are the very same elements that make up your body's physical constitution! As a matter of fact, these elements make up approximately 97% of your body's total weight!
- Your body is also composed of the same elements, minerals and gases as some of the planets in our solar system! For example, earth is composed of 30% iron, 30% oxygen, 14% magnesium, and many other elements, minerals and gases that can be found in your body. Mercury has an iron core with a silicate surface. Silica is a natural chemical compound made of silicon and oxygen which can also be found within your body. Jupiter and Saturn are almost 90% hydrogen, another elemental component of your

body. Uranus is mostly ice made up of ammonia, methane, and water, all three of which your body either produces or is naturally composed of. Your body does not only consist of these natural elements, minerals, and gases, it needs them in order to function properly!

- An adult human body is made up of approximately seven octillion atoms! Numerically that's 7,000,000,000,000,000,000,000,000,000! Each one of these atoms is a building block of your body and denotes life and energy, this can clearly be seen in the movement of the atom as the electron revolves around the nucleus core. So even down to the smallest particle of our being you can see life!

- These seven octillion atoms combine to make up over 100,000,000,000,000 (100 trillion) cells in the human body. These cells in turn combine to make up 12 major systems in the body and over 6,000 body parts!

(Your AMAZING Brain...)

- Even though all body parts are vital the brain may be considered one of the most important. Despite only weighing 2-3 pounds and taking up to only 2% of the body's mass the brain uses approximately 20% of the body's total energy and oxygen intake!

- Your brain is the "control center" for your central nervous system which is responsible for the function of every system within your body whether it is voluntary or involuntary.

- The brain sends and receives signals from the body at speeds of up to 260 miles per hour!
- While awake, your brain generates between 12 to 23 watts of power, and that is enough energy to power a light bulb!
- Within the human brain there are approximately 86 billion nerve cells joined by 100 trillion connections (synapses). This is more than the number of stars in the Milky Way! These neurons (nerve cells) can transmit 1,000 impulses per second and make tens of thousands of synaptic contacts with other neurons in the process.
- This must be why your brain is approximately 74% water! Water is needed to produce the hormones and neurotransmitters that transmit nerve impulses throughout your entire central nervous system.
- Your brain is floating! The cerebral spinal fluid that the brain floats in is mostly water and acts a shock absorber for the brain and spinal column.
- Your brain can process an image that your eyes have seen for only .13 seconds! That's faster than eye-blinking which takes .15 seconds!
- Your brain does not rest, it works 24 hours a day, 7 days a week! It has to, the natural systems, functions, and processes that it operates have to work constantly in order for us to live!

YOUR BODY'S NATUR(E)AL COMPOSITION!

To make intelligent decisions when it comes to what you eat you first have to know and understand your body's natural composition. This knowledge will help you begin to see just how interconnected you are with your environment, and the natural elements that make up our physical universe!

Fact #1:
"**Nature**" is defined as: *the physical universe*.

Fact #2:
"**Natural**" is defined as: *of or relating to **nature.***

This obviously means that everything within the physical universe, you and I included, are considered a part of "Nature", or the adjective form of the word, "Natural". There is no disputing these facts, nature is not artificial or man-made, nature is completely natural, and as a part of nature so are you!

Fact #3:
Our physical universe (nature) is mainly comprised of four **natural** elements which we also consider our "natural resources", they are:
water, earth, air, and fire (heat).

Fact #4:
Our physical body is also mainly comprised of these same four elements:
water, earth, air, and fire (heat).

Fact #5:

Outside of our body these natural elements maintain and sustain life, without them functioning in unison life as we know it could not exist.

Fact #6:

Inside of our body these elements of nature play the same vital and life-sustaining role! Our natural human body needs these natural elements within it in order to function properly, in order to live!

Fact #7:

Water provides life, it is needed within you and without you. Water comprises 92% of your blood plasma, 74% of your brain, 73% of your heart, 83% of your lungs, 64% of your skin, & 31% of your bones. It is 60% of your total body total body weight. You are **water**!

Fact #8:

Earth provides us with life in the form of food which we need for energy and cell production. The essential micronutrients it provides through plant-based proteins, fats, carbohydrates are necessary for the overall health and function of the body. You are what you eat! If I am what I eat, and the source of all foods that I eat come from the earth, this can only means that I am also in part - **earth**!

Fact #9:

Air provides us with the ATMOSPHERE in which we live! This atmosphere consists of a mixture of gases that cover the earth in a layer more than 400 miles high!

21% of this atmosphere consists of Oxygen, an element your body and brain definitely cannot do without!

Fact #10:

The **Sun/Fire** keeps all organisms alive! It is the source of energy for plants and provides us with light and heat. You are a part of the sun; your body has an almost constant temperature of 98.6 degrees!

There is no denying it, the elements of nature can clearly be seen without us, but even more extraordinary is the fact that they are also within us! Nature operates in both our physical universe and within our physical body, we are nature! This fact is <u>NOT</u> being presented to advertise or market a certain dietary regimen or way of life, it is being presented because it is truth that can help an individual build a higher level of self-respect for their body, especially when deciding what to eat!

Fact #11:

What you eat determines how you move, feel, and age!

Fact #12:

What you eat determines how your body fights disease!

The food you eat does much more than just replenish your body with energy, it also provides essential vitamins, minerals, and other nutrients that enable the cells and major systems in your body to perform their functions! The lack or deficiency of just one of these vital nutrients over time can cause your health to deteriorate and decline. For example, in order for your immune system to produce enough white blood cells to protect your body against infectious disease it needs among other things certain micronutrients such as vitamin C and Zinc. If these nutrients are not received the body's white blood cell count will begin to reduce and your immune system's ability to protect your body against sickness and disease will be compromised. **Your body's nutritional needs must be provided within the foods you eat in order for it to maintain proper health and integrity.**

This is where knowledge of self plays an important role, if you know that your body's composition is natural and operates best when it is nourished with natural and whole foods, then that is exactly what you should give it! The same goes with water, if you know that your organs are composed of mainly water, then it should be one of the main liquids that you drink! It is important to understand that your body has nutritional needs that must be met, and anything processed or made from artificial ingredients cannot supply these needs.

Fact #13:

Your body and its many systems operate best when you consume <u>whole</u> foods full of vitamins, minerals, anti-oxidants, phytochemicals, and other natural nutrients which haven't been altered, processed, or preserved.

Research is now showing that our natural body cannot properly digest anything that is artificial or has been taken out of its natural composition. For example, processed foods that contain unnatural preservatives, additives, and artificial ingredients cannot be used to provide energy to the body or aide in cellular reproduction. This means that this type of food is basically useless. Some studies are even confirming that the excess consumption of these processed foods and their ingredients are the precursors to various forms of disease and illness.

Since your body cannot digest these artificial ingredients it stores them directly in your fat cells. This is where it becomes dangerous, once they are stored in your cells they can change your cell structure and metabolize, some even become carcinogens which over time can cause cancer. These facts and the rise of disease and illnesses linked to processed foods and other artificial ingredients are making people wiser when it comes to what they eat.

Fact #14:
The food you eat plays a major role in cellular growth and development!

The process of cell production is one of the most important functions that occurs throughout your body, and the food you eat is supposed to aide it in this process, not weaken it.

Fact #15:
Out of the approximately 100 trillion cells in the human body, 300 million of them die every minute and over 300 billion are born every day!

The physical life of a human being begins as a single cell, and as this cell continues to grow and change in the first weeks of development nerve cells begin to appear. These cells keep growing and eventually help to create the body's nervous system and later its organs. The process of cellular regeneration is active and constant in every system of the body because all systems are composed of cells! Old cells are constantly being replaced by new cells, this process continues your entire life time and only slows with old-age. What is absolutely vital to understand is that the power behind this entire process of cellular development and growth is the food you eat because the nutrients found within it helps determine the health and quality of your body's cells.

Fact #16:
YOU ARE WHAT **YOU DECIDE** TO EAT!

As mentioned before, cells make up every system and part of your body. For example, there are bone cells, liver cells, skin cells, muscle cells, blood cells, etc. These cells all have different lifespans and are eventually replaced by new cells of its own kind. The food you eat is the main source of energy needed to produce these new cells. **This means that the cells produced from what YOU DECIDE to eat eventually become the new cells or building blocks of your body.**

An easy way to understand cell regeneration or production is by knowing the ages of different cells that comprise different parts of your body. The list below gives you an approximate age of different body parts and the length it takes for them to completely regenerate (renew itself).

Body Part:	Lifespan: (regeneration time)
Intestinal lining	3-5 days
Full finger nail	6 months (to grow a full nail)
Red Blood Cells	4 months

Skin surface(epidermis)	2-4 weeks
Taste buds	10-14 days
Lungs	2-3 weeks

It is absolutely amazing, on a cellular level the vast majority of your body parts and organs completely regenerate themselves over time, and you determine the health of these new cells used in the renewing process by what you choose to eat! This means that each time you eat is a new opportunity to build a healthier body, a healthier you! The "natural processes" (organ function, cell production, digestion, etc.) that happen throughout your body need natural nutrients in order to maintain and sustain an optimal level of operation. The best sources for these nutrients are whole foods still in their natural state such as: fresh fruits, vegetables, nuts, seeds, whole grains, beans, legumes, and lentils (just to name a few). These types of foods contain the vitamins, minerals, anti-oxidants, and other nutrients needed for proper digestion, energy use, and cell production. Your body can understand and utilize these foods best because they are unaltered, whole, and full of natural nutrients.

You have the power to manage your own physical health by what you decide to eat, and the more you know and respect your body's natural composition the more intelligent this decision-making process will be. Eating is a voluntary action, I know that might sound obvious **but there are many people suffering from illnesses that stem directly from what they <u>voluntarily</u> decide** to put in their mouth! You control this action! Nobody forces you to eat anything, it is you that picks what food to eat, places it in your mouth, chews it, and swallows it! Poor nutrition is considered as eating foods that lack the proper nutritional qualities the body needs to function at an optimal level. It is directly linked to symptoms and illnesses such as high blood pressure, high cholesterol, diabetes, tooth decay, heart disease, obesity, strokes, osteoporosis and other ailments that impair your health and well-being.

What is fantastic to know about this entire process or action of eating is that you are in total control of it! It is simply a matter of using your will-power and the knowledge of your natural composition to make the right food choices that will provide your body with the nutrients needed to maintain an optimal state of health.

As we conclude this section on the body and begin discussing the power of your mind, it will become more evident to you that every physical action starts first with a thought, and if you can control this thought you can determine the action it produces and its result. This is how you begin to shape your own destiny and manage your own health, by utilizing your will and the power of your mind to create your own genuine reality and level of well-being.

Chapter 3:
THE POWER OF YOUR MIND!

The **power of your mind** is two-fold, it has the power to receive and give commands. The commands that it <u>receives</u> comes from your **intentions** and **will-power**, and the commands it <u>gives</u> directs your **body, actions**, and **words** to follow your *will-power* until your original *intention* is accomplished. This is the process needed in order to shape your own destiny, and each step in this process includes components of your being that you are directly in control of. You create your own **intentions** and **goals**, you utilize your own **will-power**, you control your own **mind** and **thought process**, you tell your **body** what **movements** and **actions** to perform, and you are responsible for whatever the **effects** and **consequences** are, which end up determining if you accomplished your original **intent** or **goal** in the first place! If you do not take an active role in this process of shaping your own destiny, you may create a future for yourself full of issues and problems that could have been avoided.

Before we go any further into discussing the **power of your mind** take a good look at the formula below, it provides each component in the process of "shaping your own destiny" and what they represent...

<u>Intention</u>	+	<u>Will-power</u>	+	<u>Mind</u>	+	<u>Body</u>	=	<u>Results!</u>
Goals/Aims		Energy/Drive		Thought Process		Movement		Goal
Objectives		Inspiration		Control Center		Action/Word		achieved?

As we begin discussing the **power of your mind** let's take a more in-depth look at the two components it utilizes to operate and function, your **intention** and **will-power**!

"Intention" is defined as:

> 1) A determination to act in a certain way.
> 2) The end or object intended; Purpose.
> 3) A specific goal, aim, intent, or objective.

Your "intentions" are composed of your personal or professional goals, aims, and objectives, they help fuel your will-power and provide your life with purpose, inspiration, and a sense of determination. Your intentions also provide the blueprints and guidelines that your **will-power** follows to ensure that you reach your goals and objectives. If you do not know what you **intend** to do with your life and you have no personal or professional goals, then now is the best time to create some! Setting realistic goals in your life increases your will-power, a lack of them diminishes it. (Chapter 6 provides you with an opportunity to set personal and professional goals)

"Will-power" is defined as:

> The ability to control yourself and determine your own actions, thoughts, and feelings.

Your **will-power** receives inspiration once you know and understand what you **intend** to do with your life. It then begins to empower your **mind** with the energy needed to move, think, feel, speak, and do other things necessary in order to fulfill whatever your intent, purpose, or objective is.

Will-power develops self-discipline through the power of forced physical, mental, and emotional repetition. Whatever you tell yourself to do, think, or feel repeatedly you will become more disciplined at doing, thinking, and feeling.

Those same actions, thoughts, and emotions that you are telling yourself to do, think, or feel will produce consequences and effects that either strengthen or weaken you. This is how good or bad habits are formed, this is also how you begin to shape your own destiny or become your own worst enemy, it all depends on what your **intent** is and what you are **willing** yourself to do with the power of your mind and actions. It's all up to you!

"**Mind**" is defined as:

The part of an individual that feels, perceives, <u>thinks</u>, wills, and reasons.

In this section we are going to deal with the part of your mind that "thinks", also known as your "thought process". This component of your **mind** is important to understand because it uses a tremendous amount of your personal energy intake. The average adult mind thinks between 15,000 to 50,000 thoughts per day, and energy follows each one of these thoughts! If we take the average of these two numbers (32,500 thought per day) and divide it by the 16 hours of the day in which the average person is awake it comes out to approximately 2,000 thoughts per hour, 30 thoughts per minute, and 1 thought every 2 seconds! That is a lot of thoughts, as a matter of fact, that is too many thoughts! The best way to strengthen the **power of your mind** is by reducing this excessive number of thoughts, especially the ones that have no relevance or effect your being in a negative way. The energy saved from reducing unnecessary thoughts can be used for more high priority things in your life such as your personal growth, family, friends, hobbies, or profession.

Provided below are 3 specific **"powers of your mind"** that you must know and understand if you want to take more control of your thought process and shape your own destiny:

(1st Power of your MIND)

Energy follows every thought that you have! Where ever your thought goes, your energy follows! This is not theory, it is how your mind and thoughts naturally function. To give just one example, if energy did not follow our thoughts then we would not be able to voluntarily move or speak, these actions begin first with a thought! Thinking requires energy because it in part uses the faculties of your brain, and as stated earlier your tiny brain in comparison with your overall body uses up to 20% of all energy and oxygen intake. If you look at how much we move and how much we speak you can clearly see why our brain uses so much of our energy.

The process of thinking is obviously very important, but 15,000 to 50,000 thoughts per day certainly include thoughts which are unnecessary, waste precious energy, and produce a negative state of mind that can be harmful to your entire being. We all have them, thoughts that deal with unnecessary and unwarranted stress, anxiety, fear, guilt, shame, addictions, relationship issues, past trauma, health issues, etc. These are the wrong types of thoughts to put your precious energy into because they not only effect you but also your family, friends, job, and other relationships as well. The good thing to know is that these thoughts and the negative energy/actions they produce can be reduced over time and eventually eliminated by utilizing the **power of your mind**.

One of the best self-given methods for reducing these useless and harmful thoughts in order to save your energy and utilize it for more relevant purposes is by **training your mind**! Just like the body your mind can also be exercised and made more efficient through the practice of concentration. The process of training your mind involves a simple 5-minute **mind-body exercise** which involves focusing your thought and attention on the rise and fall of your chest as you breathe. This exercise is simple, requires no equipment, and can be done anywhere and anytime. It reduces the number of thoughts you have by simply giving your mind a single point of focus to concentrate on, your breath. According to the above numbers an average adult thinks approximately 150 thoughts in 5 minutes. This means that by utilizing this simple 5-minute mind-body exercise you can reduce 150 scattered thoughts into 1 powerful thought which focuses all its energy back into you! This exercise not only reduces your thoughts it also helps lower stress which is cited by doctors and researchers as a major contributor to many different illnesses of the body and mind such as heart disease, high blood pressure, PTSD, and depression.

(2nd Power of your MIND)

There is a thought before every movement you make and word you speak! Both of these actions require the use of your muscular system which receives all commands from your brain through your nervous system. Your muscular system is comprised of **voluntary muscle** that enables your body to move and speak, and **involuntary muscle** like heart muscle and smooth muscle which operate automatic functions within your body such as your cardiovascular and digestive systems. This means that the involuntary action of your heart beat and the voluntary action of simply lifting your arm are both controlled by your brain. In this section we are dealing with your voluntary muscles, they are the ones that put your destiny in your own hands because it is **YOU** that control them!

This might sound easy to understand but most people go through their entire life and don't realize that every word they speak and movement they make is controlled by their thought. The ultra-speed (200-260mph) at which the brain sends and receives signals from the body, and its ability to send numerous signals almost at the same time so we can move and speak is so fast that we sometimes are not aware these actions are controlled. To see your thought actually controlling your movement and words you simply have to slow them down. The following mind-body exercises should be performed at least once in your life time, they show you the amazing connection between your mind and body.

Mind-body Exercise #1: "Mindful movement"
(read through the exercise before starting)
Choose a body part to observe and for the next 60 seconds move it **very slowly** in different directions. During the entire 60 seconds keep your focus and attention on the chosen body part, observe how it moves according to the direction in which your mind tells it to. For example, place your hand

in front of you and begin to move it in different ways **very slowly**.

Reflection:

Could you observe your mind moving this body part?
Could you observe the thought before the action?

Mind-body Exercise #2: "Minding Your Words"
(read through the exercise before starting)

Phase 1: To do this exercise you have to choose something that is already a part of your memory. Close your eyes to avoid distractions and with an audible voice say your full name, date of birth, and place of birth **very slowly**. Try and speak so slow that you are almost sounding out each letter in each word. As you are **slowly** speaking, see if you can observe the words in your thoughts before you actually speak them out.

Reflection:

Were you able to see the words in your thoughts before you spoke them?
Could you see the thoughts come before the words as you were speaking slowly?

Phase 2: Repeat the same process as before, but this time keep your focus on your lips and tongue so you can observe the many movements they make in order to form the words you are speaking. Each one of these movements starts with a thought!

Could you observe the many different movements that your tongue and lips make in order to form your words?
Could you see your mind controlling the muscles involved with speaking?

If there is a thought before every movement you make and word you speak, then **what are you telling yourself to do and say**? Your future health and physical fitness are defined by how you decide to move today! For example, if eating is an action in which you voluntarily put food into your mouth, chew, and swallow it, then **what are you telling yourself to eat**? This decision is completely under your control and has tremendous consequences. As discussed earlier, what you eat determines how you move, feel, and age. It also determines the overall health of your cells and how your body will fight disease in the future! Eating is an action that you control which means that your health is ultimately in your hands! **The key to controlling what you eat is in the thought process which precedes the action of eating**. Having respect for your body and a knowledge of its natural composition, processes, and nutritional needs enables you to make healthier and more intelligent choices when deciding what to eat!

Your level of physical fitness is also completely up to you. Physical fitness requires movement, and before every movement there is a thought, so **how are you telling yourself to move,** or more importantly, **are you telling yourself to move at all**? All physical movement of the body starts with the brain which in turn is controlled by the **power of your mind**. Voluntary movement and repetition in the form of manual labor or fitness provides numerous benefits to your overall health. At the same time, it can help reduce your chances of developing diseases that occur much more often in people who move very little or not at all. Keep in mind that the strength of your individual will-power is determined by your intent. **Do you intend to be fit? Is it your intention, goal or aim to have a strong body and heart?** If you make it your goal, aim, and objective to become more physically fit then your will-power will follow, "where there is a will, there is a way".

Performing some type of physical fitness is not the only "voluntary" movement necessary in life that you have control over. You should also have other personal and professional goals that require you to use your will-power, mind, body, words, and actions to accomplish. Whether it is furthering your education, getting promoted, losing weight, changing your diet, or simply reading a book, everybody should have at least one goal, aim, or objective that they want to reach in their life. It comes back to the question of intent. What do you intend to do with yourself? Are you happy with where you are physically, mentally, emotionally, socially, financially, and professionally? If not, then **what are you telling yourself to do in order to change your circumstances?**

Most goals have tasks or duties that must be accomplished daily if you want to reach them, and this obviously requires voluntary thinking and movement that you control. For example, if you want to get a degree you have to go to class, do your homework, study for tests, and accomplish all the preliminary requirements necessary to receive it. Your destiny is shaped by what you decide to do today! The only person possible of stopping you from fulfilling your dreams or ambitions is you. As stated earlier, your destiny is determined by how **YOU DECIDE** to move, think, and feel <u>today</u>.

(3rd Power of your MIND)

The last "power of the mind" that we will discuss is probably the most powerful of all, it includes the ability to change any mental or emotional state by utilizing the power of your thought and the "**Law of Polarity**" (or opposites). The term for this process is called **Mental Transmutation**. Before we go into detail on how it works let us first define the two terms involved in the process...

"Transmutation" is defined as:

To change from one nature, substance, form, or condition into another; To transform.

A good example of transmutation would be to take a pot of room- temperature water and place it on a hot stove top, eventually the water would begin to rise in temperature and be "transmuted" or changed into hot water. The power behind this transmutation from room-temperature water to hot water was the focused heat energy of the stove top, if you remove the hot water from the heat it will eventually transmute or change back into room-temperature water. **Transmutation is the change or transformation from one nature, substance, form, or condition into another**.

The art of "**mental**" **transmutation** works in the same way, it uses the ability of your will-power and focused thought to transform negative mental or emotional states into more positive and balanced ones. This is done by willing your mind to think on the **opposite** of the thought or emotion you want to change. This forced redirection of your thought shifts the energy away from the negative aspect, and channels it into the positive aspect until a healthy balance is achieved.

The universal law that is used to perform mental transmutation is the "Law of Polarity". The principles included within the **"Law of Polarity"** state that:

**-Everything in life is dual in nature
and has two parts;**

-Everything has two aspects or poles;

**-Everything has its pair of opposites that
differ only in degree.**

A few examples of this principle include terms like: hot/cold, up/down, love/hate, left/right, positive/ negative, high/low, sharp/dull or courage/fear. Even though these terms may be opposites they are still on the same pole and only differ in degree. The law of polarity does not work with things that are not opposites because they are not on the same pole, for example, hot/down, up/cold, or left/hate are not polar opposites and cannot be transmuted with each other. To clearly understand this principle, look at the diagram given below that shows the direct relationship between the two polar terms of "love" and "hate".

<u>Love | Hate</u>

Love---------|------------|-------------|------------|----------|-----------**Hate**

| Like | Like a | Neither | Don't | Strongly |
| a lot | little | | like | dislike |

In this diagram you can see that love and hate are on the same pole and vary only in degrees, even though they are extreme opposites. This means that with the power of your will and mind you can use the "law of polarity" to **mentally transmute** vibrations of hate into vibrations of love. Remember, **energy follows every thought that you have**, so if you redirect your thought from things you hate into things that you love your energy will follow. The same goes with any other mental or emotional vibrations you want to transform, you can change thoughts of fear into thoughts of courage, or feelings of sadness into feelings of happiness. Any negative mental or emotional state can be changed or transmuted into its opposite state of positivity. **Mental transmutation is self-medication for the mind that is yours to use at any time.** If you use it on a regular basis it can increase the power of your mind to the point where you can change a negative thought into a positive one in the blink of an eye!

Your mental and emotional well-being are determined by you! YOU DECIDE how you think and eventually become what you think. YOU DECIDE how you feel and eventually your actions and words show how you feel. Yes, there are outside influences that can have a negative effect on how you think or feel, but in the end, it is YOU that decides whether you hold these thoughts and feelings or mentally transmute them into better ones.

Chapter 4:
YOUR EMOTIONS

Your emotions when activated produce impulses (signals/vibrations) which are interpreted by your mind and displayed through your words and actions. Your mind receives theses impulses that come from your unchecked or negative emotions and reacts to them by producing certain physiological changes in your body such as a rapid heartbeat, an increase or decrease in your breath rate, or even more dangerous the over-activation or deactivation of your glands.

The constant repetition of these physiological changes due to the unchecked emotions that stimulate them can cause your body's internal systems to weaken and malfunction. A rapid heart rate is no different than a mini heart-attack because it adds unwarranted stress to your heart and lowers its capacity to function properly, a decrease in breath rate lowers the amount of oxygenated blood to the brain which can result in several different malfunctions within your body, and anything that causes your glands not to properly function is dangerous because they are responsible for producing the hormones and chemical messengers that help regulate most of your bodily functions.

To avoid these types of physiological changes you first have to understand the emotions which cause them. True healing begins by dealing with the source of the imbalance or dis-ease, and most of the time it originates with mismanaged emotions that constantly reoccur and eventually have a negative effect and influence on your mental and physical health. For example, some people are "emotional eaters" which means that in response to negative or mismanaged emotions they increase their food intake, and most of the time it is unhealthy snack foods that are either high in sodium, refined sugar, or artificial ingredients. This unnecessary increase in eating due to an unchecked or misunderstood emotion can over time cause physical issues such as obesity, diabetes, or high blood pressure. These physical ailments can then lead to forms of mental ailments like depression, grief, low self-esteem, or anxiety. In order to experience a more complete healing you have to consider the health of your body, mind, and emotions, a positive or negative change in any one of these components of your being can quickly affect the other.

Despite how hard it may be at times to control your emotions it does not stop the fact that there is still a **thought before every word you speak and movement you make**. This means that regardless of how strong your feelings are it is still **YOU** that decides how to express them. You act according to how you feel, so any emotion that **YOU DECIDE** to hold onto will eventually reveal itself through your words and actions. Some emotions come and go quickly, but those that you **willingly** hold can produce moods or mind-sets that have a negative effect on you and the people around you. It is important to know that how you feel effects how you think, and how you think reflects how you feel. If you think negative thoughts you will eventually produce negative feelings, and on the other hand, if you harbor or hold negative feelings you will eventually produce negative thoughts.

Mental transmutation works with your **emotions** as well because they are reflected in your thoughts, but for it to function you first have to know <u>what</u> emotions you are feeling and <u>why</u> you are feeling them, this is called **emotional awareness**. It is difficult to transmute or change a feeling if you don't first face it and try to understand why you feel that way. Being aware of your feelings when they occur can help you determine the root cause of the emotion and what stimulates it. Once you confront what caused the emotion to surface you then can use your thought process to logically confront it and transmute it. For example, if you experience something in your life that creates an angry emotional reaction you first must understand **why** the experience made you angry. Once you know and understand what caused the anger to surface you can begin to take more control of your emotional reaction to it by choosing when, where, and how to express it. Building an emotional awareness allows you to understand how you feel so you can better manage your feelings. Some emotions, if expressed in the wrong way, at the wrong time, or in the wrong place can cause you to regret your actions and words or make it even more difficult to resolve a problem.

It is important to understand that both positive and negative emotions are normal, what matters is how you manage and express them. Your emotions provide information about you, they reveal how you feel about daily experiences in your life by the emotional reactions they produce. These experiences help you make better decisions on how to express these emotions when they resurface.

Getting upset with yourself for feeling a certain emotion does not help you deal with the emotion or it's cause, even an emotion like sadness can help you understand yourself better once you know what causes it.

How other people feel also plays a role in how you feel. The more sensitive, empathetic, and nonjudgmental you are toward other people's emotions the easier it will be for you to maintain your emotional balance. Having the ability to get along with people helps you in almost every area of your life, and the only way to do this is by becoming more aware of your emotions and what causes them so you can find the best way to express them.

Provided in the list below are tips that can help you become more aware and intelligent when dealing with your emotions. These guidelines will help you understand your emotions better so you can manage them properly and maintain emotional stability.

1. TRACK YOUR EMOTIONS!

Pick an emotion that you might have problems managing or expressing and try your best to track it all day. When you notice that you are feeling it make a mental note, write it down, or send yourself a text message with the name of the emotion and what caused it to surface. Towards the end of the day either refer to your mental notes, written log, or phone to reflect on the emotion that you tracked that day. Over time this will help you become more aware of your emotions when you are feeling them, it is a great way to understand what you are feeling and why you are feeling it.

The more aware you are of the emotion the more intelligent you can become at managing and expressing it! (The best method to use when tracking your emotions is to write them down, the information you accumulate could eventually become an emotional "log" or "journal" that you can always refer to when dealing with your emotions)

2. GROW YOUR GRATITUDE!

Gratitude is simply being thankful and appreciative for the things that you have in life, too include life itself! You can express your gratitude by taking the time to reflect on how fortunate you are when good things happen in your life, even the small ones. Showing gratitude on a daily basis strengthens your ability to maintain mental and emotional balance. It helps focus your attention on things you are grateful for and appreciate which in turn helps shift energy away from more harmful feelings like sadness, disappointment, loneliness, or grief. Love and gratitude are the best emotions to use in order to transmute or change negative emotional states.

There are so many things in life to be thankful for: a sunny day, waking up in the morning, clean water, friends and family, your health. Find the things you are personally thankful for and make it a priority of yours to show your gratitude and appreciation for them on a daily or weekly basis. Creating a "Gratitude Journal" is the best way to do this, a constant reminder of the things you are thankful for will help you maintain a positive and optimistic attitude. The best method for creating a gratitude journal is by using your cell phone, everybody has one! Simply use the "reminder" or "calendar" app in your phone to create a daily or weekly alarm that reminds you of the things you are grateful for. To ensure that this works take at least 5 minutes to reflect on these things every time the alarm or reminder goes off. As you are reflecting, add another thing you are thankful for to the reminder until you have accumulated a journal full of things that help you express your gratitude. This brief 5 minutes that you take to count your blessings can turn a seemingly gloomy day into a happy one!

3. DON'T LET OTHER PEOPLES WORDS OR ACTIONS EFFECT YOU!

This is easier said than done, but that doesn't mean it can't be learned, developed, and mastered. It starts by always keeping in mind that **YOU DECIDE** how you feel, regardless of the circumstances or what other people around you are doing or saying. You are not responsible for anyone's words or actions, **you are only responsible for how you react to them.** The best way to defend against negative emotions, words, or actions that come from other people is by remaining sensitive, nonjudgmental, and patient with them. Expressing empathy is another way to provide support to someone who might be dealing with a problem or lack of emotional self-control. It involves taking the time to place yourself in the other person's position in order to share their feelings, understand them better, and hopefully provide the necessary support and encouragement they need to regain their balance.

You can still love and care for someone and not necessarily love what they say or do. The longer you let other people's actions and words affect you the more difficult it becomes to maintain your own emotional stability. **How can you work on your own emotional weak-points if you are constantly worried and consumed with the things that other people are doing or saying**? The most effective way to help change someone is by first changing yourself. Nobody is perfect, we all have things in our life that need to be worked on and developed if we want to better ourselves and optimize our well-being. Learn to take a closer look at your own mistakes and forgive the shortcomings of others, showing mercy and compassion is better than constant judgement and ridicule. You also must have patience with yourself! Admitting your own mistakes and learning to forgive yourself is vital if you want to maintain emotional stability and continue to progress in life.

4. ACTIVATING YOUR RELAXATION RESPONSE!

Trying not to let what other people do or say affect you is sometimes more difficult when it comes to friends and family, but it is still important to follow this guideline for your own sake and those you are close to. If a problem or issue surfaces and you begin to feel like the situation is too much for you to handle it can trigger your nervous system to activate your "fight or flight" (stress) response. This is a natural defense mechanism of your body's nervous system that is activated when you perceive yourself to be in a life-threatening situation. It causes many physiological changes that prepares your body to either run from perceived danger or fight to stay alive. Even though this "fight or flight" response is natural, it shouldn't be activated unless the situation is life-threatening or requires you to perform under extreme pressure or circumstances. An argument with a friend or family member is **not** life-threatening, a problem at work is **not** life-threatening, what other people say to you (even if it causes some pain or disappointment) is **not** life-threatening, so you should try your best **not** to treat these types of situations as such. The constant activation of your stress response, especially when the situation is not life-threatening can cause unnecessary damage to your body and mind that is difficult to reverse.

Some people handle stress better than others, for those who have more difficulty dealing with stressful situations hope is not lost. The best method to combat stress and maintain emotional balance is by voluntarily activating your **"relaxation response"**. This is a form of self-medication or self-treatment that can be used to prevent the onset of stress or reverse its effects almost immediately. Just like the stress response it is also a built-in mechanism of your nervous system, but instead of preparing your body for perceived danger it does the opposite by sending signals to your brain that calm your body down, reverse the physiological changes brought on by the stress, and help shift your energy back to the vital systems and organs that need it. **The extraordinary thing about your "relaxation response" is that it is always at your disposal, you just have to voluntarily activate it**!

There are several different Mind-Body Exercises that can be used to activate your relaxation response, but the most efficient method is by utilizing the power of your **breath**! Your breath is a natural tranquilizer for your mind and body, as soon as you focus your attention on your breathing and begin to control its rhythm it automatically triggers your nervous system to activate your relaxation response! This is exactly why breathing exercises are one of the most effective methods to use in order to reverse the onset and effects of stress, they work almost immediately!

Your breath can be used in this way because it is both a part of your voluntary and involuntary nervous systems. This means that you can voluntarily make yourself breathe when you want to (like when performing breathing exercises), and your body also involuntarily breathes on its own (like when sleeping). **Your breath is the bridge or connection that links the voluntary and involuntary parts of your nervous system together.** If used consistently, certain breathing exercises and the relaxing rhythms they produce can be used to diminish chronic stress and prevent your body from engaging your stress response during situations that are not life-threatening.

Provided below is an example of a Breathing Exercise that can be used at any time to help you deal with a difficult situation or reverse the effects of stress. The more consistent you are at using this breathing exercise to activate your relaxation response the stronger you will be when it comes to conquering stress and managing your emotions.

<u>Breathing Exercise</u> - **Mindful Breathing**
Making your breath "Deeper, Quieter, and Slower"

Take a couple of breaths and focus your attention on the rise and fall of your chest as you inhale and exhale. Once your mind is focused on your breathing begin to make each breath deeper, quieter, and slower. (keep in mind that you want to gradually make your breathing deeper, quieter, and slower with each breath, not all at once! Take it one breath at a time)

This simple breathing exercise can be used even if you are in the middle of a difficult or stressful situation, it may help you find the solution to the problem or at the least help keep your emotions in check! Practicing these types of breathing exercises on a daily basis can greatly benefit your mind, body, and emotions. The most important component needed to reap the full benefits of these breathing exercises is simple repetition. The more you repeat a process the better you become at it, if you maintain the repetition with consistency and regularity you can eventually master it. You can start by practicing this breathing exercise for 5 minutes a day, once you begin to feel the positive effects and are more comfortable with it you can lengthen the time of your sessions to 10 minutes or simply add another 5-minute session to your day. The small amount of time spent practicing this self-healing exercise will have a positive effect by helping you to think and act more clearly as you handle all the problems, situations, or challenges that come your way.

In concluding this chapter, it is important to reiterate a few important facts that you should always keep in mind when it comes to your body, mind, and emotions...

You are what **YOU DECIDE** to eat,
You become what **YOU DECIDE** to think, &
You act on how **YOU DECIDE** to feel!

YOUR DESTINY, HEALTH, AND HAPPINESS
IS IN YOUR HANDS,

You truly are the Master of your own fate, whether you
know it or not!

Chapter 5:
An Introduction to Integrative Medicine

Note to reader: Before beginning any form of medication please consult a professional in the field of medicine you have chosen to follow or practice! This is only an introduction to Integrative Medicine, if you do not fully understand a component that you are interested in then consult a professional and do your own research before beginning anything on your own. Information is power, know and understand it before you do it!

Integrative Medicine encompasses all forms of medicine from modern-day "conventional" medicine to more non-mainstream "alternative" forms of medicine. It is sometimes referred to as "whole person" (or holistic) medicine because it treats the physical, mental, and emotional dimensions of an individual so a more complete healing can take place. Integrative Medicine is also considered "intelligent medicine" because it does not exclude any form of therapy, treatment, or health-care, especially if it is natural in its approach and promotes healing.

There are numerous methods and techniques of healing that fall under "Integrative Medicine", but we will focus on those that specifically deal with you! To utilize most forms of medicine a licensed practitioner, doctor, or physician is required, but there are some variations of Integrative medicine that are considered as forms of self-medication or self-treatment. These are the methods and techniques we will discuss, those that only require your will-power and the proper use of your own natural energy resources.

Before we go into more detail about these specific components of Integrative Medicine that are directly related to you, it is important to provide a brief overview of its main definition and principles. To do this I will start this chapter with a short summary of each topic that will be discussed, this will provide you with a preview of how vast the field of Integrative Medicine is and how its philosophy involves a natural and genuine approach to making a healthier and happier you!

In this chapter we will discuss…
1. Integrative Medicine's overall definition.
2. Integrative Medicine's main principle - YOU!
3. Specific **Principles** of Integrative Medicine related to you!
> **a**. Homeostasis (life-balance)–The natural healing potential of your body, mind, and emotions.
> **b**. Prevention! – Stop and THINK before you do and say!
> **c**. Natural Energy Production–Empowering your voluntary nervous system.
4. Mind-body Exercise – A form of Self-Medication!
> **a**. Mind-body exercise – The ultimate power of your breath!
> **b**. Intro to exercises - Breathing Meditations (exercise) & Guided Imagery
> **c**. Meditational Fitness

1. Integrative Medicine's Overall Definition

The first thing to understand about Integrative Medicine is that it is not just one form of medicine, it is a **combination** of utilizing both "Conventional" and "Alternative" forms of medicine to help someone heal. For example, someone taking over-the-counter pain medication (conventional medicine) prescribed by their doctor for back pain could also be receiving acupuncture (alternative medicine) for the very same pain. It then could be said that this person is utilizing a form of "Integrative Medicine" to heal because they are using **both** modern (Conventional) and non-modern (Alternative) forms of medicine to induce healing. They are "integrating" different forms of medicines, treatments, and health-care approaches as long as they are relevant and accommodate healing. Other examples of "Integrative Medicine" could include:

-Utilizing Progressive Muscle Relaxation to help expedite the healing from a surgical procedure.

-Utilizing Breathing Exercises along with doctor prescribed medications to reduce chronic stress.

-Utilizing Guided Imagery along with over-the-counter medication to reduce PTSD.

Since Integrative Medicine encompasses both "conventional" and "alternative" forms of medicine I have provided a very brief description of each below.

Conventional (or Modern) Medicine is one of the most commonly practiced forms of medicine used today in America and Europe. The top priority of conventional medicine is to diagnose the disease or illness of the patient. The next priority is then to treat the symptoms and disease of the patient utilizing either over-the-counter medication, radiation, or surgery. In certain emergency situations like a stroke or heart-attack the process of Conventional Medicine can save lives. Other names for this type of medicine include:

modern medicine, allopathic medicine, western medicine, orthodox medicine, or mainstream medicine.

Alternative (or Complementary) Medicine is considered any non-conventional form of medicine, therapy, or treatment that is being used **instead of** conventional or modern medicine. There are numerous forms of "alternative" medicine and all are intended to either strengthen an individual's overall being or help bring about healing and balance. Some of the more commonly known forms of **Alternative Medicine** include:

-Alternative Medical systems such as Traditional Chinese Medicine, Ayurvedic medicine, Naturopathic Medicine, Preventive medicine...

-Body-based Therapies such as Osteopathic therapy, Chiropractic therapy, Reflexology, Massage therapy...

-Energy-based Therapies such as Mind-body Exercise which includes Guided Imagery, Progressive Muscle Relaxation, Breathing Meditation (exercise), Relaxation Therapy...

-Exercise-based Therapies such as Yoga, Tai-chi, Mindful Walking/Jogging, Meditational Fitness...

Each one of these various forms of medicines, treatments, and therapies are considered Alternative medicine. If these very same "alternative" forms of medicine are given in conjunction **with** conventional medicine, then they are considered "Complementary" medicine. There is absolutely no difference between alternative and complementary medicine, the former is used **instead of** conventional medicine (Alternative), and the latter is used **in combination with** conventional medicine (Complementary). These days both alternative and complementary medicine are referred to by the acronym "CAM".

As you continue keep in mind that Integrative Medicine is a combination of utilizing both conventional and alternative forms of medicine in a coordinated way to help an individual heal. It makes use of all appropriate therapies, especially if they are evidence-based, non-invasive, and have been proven to help a person regain their physical, mental, or emotional health.

2. Integrative Medicine's Main Principle – YOU!

If you want to heal a dis-ease or imbalance and make yourself whole again you must take all parts of your being into consideration. **Integrative Medicine** does this by placing **YOU** in the center and looking at all major aspects of your life (physical, mental, emotional, personal, professional, environmental) that could possibly influence your health, and addresses any imbalances found so a more complete healing can take place.

All components of your being are integrated, work together, influence each other, and have a direct effect on your quality of life. This means that you should take each of these components into consideration when trying to attain and maintain an optimal level of health and well-being. An imbalance in one aspect of your being can easily lead to pain, discomfort, or disease in another aspect of your being.

3. Specific Principles of Int. Medicine Related to You!

There are many principles of Integrative medicine that relate to you as a natural human being. These principles provide important and vital information about how your body and its many systems naturally operate and function. We have already covered some of these subjects in previous chapters. In this section I have added three more important principles that are directly related to you, the more you know about them the better you will understand self!

3a. Homeostasis "life-balance"

This term is in part defined as your body's natural ability and desire to maintain balance, integrity, and wholeness. An obvious example of this is if you cut yourself or break a bone, your body's natural state of integrity or wholeness is temporarily lost, and it begins to mend, repair, and heal itself until it eventually regains its original state of integrity and wholeness. Your body does this because it has an innate pull or tendency to be whole and its many systems are designed to help it maintain this natural level of integrity.

Another good example of homeostasis is your body's ability to maintain its proper temperature. When your body is too hot it begins to sweat in order to cool itself down. On the other hand, if your body becomes too cold it begins to shiver in order to produce heat and warm itself up! Your body has an amazing ability and need to maintain a level of integrity and wholeness so it can function properly, and this state of being is referred to as homeostasis.

This is also true of your mental and emotional states as well, they also desire balance and harmony, but to harmonize or bring balance to these components of your being it requires more individual will-power and self-discipline. As explained in the previous chapter, it is only through a process of learning how to **mentally transmute** or change negative thoughts and emotions into more positive energies that true balance and health can be attained on a mental or emotional level.

Knowing that your body, mind, and emotions naturally seek to be balanced and whole is inspiring for those who might be suffering from pain or discomfort. It helps to understand that despite whatever illness or disease you might have, your body, mind, and emotions are always working together to combat it in order to regain their original state of health and happiness. What is even more extraordinary is that you have the ability to expedite this natural healing process by how you choose to utilize your body, mind, and emotions.

3b. <u>PREVENTION!</u>

Preventive Medicine, also known as "Prevention", is a component of Integrative Medicine that promotes activities and exercises which help to prevent the onset or occurrence of disease. It does this in part by providing vital information and natural guidelines that help you make more intelligent life-style decisions when it comes to how you act, think, and feel. Listed below are some of the many principles and guidelines found within the concept of "Prevention" that are specifically related to you:

-Preventions main objectives is to teach you how to **STOP** and **THINK** before you do or say things that can create dis-ease or imbalance in your life and threaten your future health and well-being. Your decisions decide your destiny!

-Prevention helps you find the root cause of an imbalance or disease so you can treat it properly AND take the necessary steps to ensure that it will not return. For example, conventional medicine might prescribe over-the-counter medication when someone is diagnosed with high blood pressure, regardless of what caused it to rise. Preventive Medicine takes a slightly different approach, it looks at what might have caused the blood pressure to rise in the first place (stress, diet, circumstance) and deals specifically with these issues in order to ensure that it does not reoccur or resurface. If stress caused it to rise then you deal with what is causing the stress, if diet was the cause then you deal with that aspect. **Prevention helps you find the root cause of a dis-ease or imbalance so you can start the healing process exactly where the illness began!**

-Prevention guidelines provide information on the importance of cutting **excess** (too much of one thing is good for nothing!) It also does the opposite by shedding light on **deficiencies** which can become just as dangerous to your health as excess can. Just to give a couple examples: **excess** consumption of salt and sugar is causing an increase in the number of people diagnosed with illnesses such as obesity, diabetes, high blood pressure, high cholesterol, and other avoidable ailments. An example of a **deficiency** that causes many health issues is the refusal of people to drink water!

This voluntary and ignorant deficiency leads to many different health issues which can be avoided or PREVENTED by simply drinking more water! **Prevention requires you to find your own personal excesses and deficiencies in order to bring them into balance so unnecessary dis-ease or illness can be avoided.**

-Prevention guidelines provide an absolute method for problem-solving. It instructs that **every problem has a solution**. The key is to find the solution and utilize it!

The practice of Prevention requires an individual to admit their weak-points (to themselves) and start the process of working to make them stronger and more balanced.

-The practice of Prevention requires an individual to come face to face with things that create sadness, guilt, shame, fear, or unnecessary stress in their life. If these thoughts and feelings are allowed to go unchecked they can produce certain physiological changes to your body that over time can produce dis-ease or illness.

-The practice of Prevention means making a constant effort to keep your actions, thoughts, and words in unison with what is good, clean, and natural. **Right thinking, right feeling, and right actions produce RIGHTEOUS results!**

Prevention deals specifically with how to strengthen and refine a person in order to help them prevent the onset or occurrence of disease in their life. It does this by positively forcing a person to become more mindful of the things they do and say. Practicing Prevention also requires a certain level of self-respect, if you have respect for your body and understand its natural composition you will make more intelligent decisions when it comes to what you do with it, what you feed it, and how you maintain it!

The best way to begin the practice of Prevention is by performing Mind-body exercises like Breath-work (Breathing Exercises & Meditations) or Guided Imagery. These exercises increase your body's ability to prevent disease by utilizing the **natural forms of energy** produced through your voluntary nervous system to access, strengthen, and heal your involuntary nervous system.

In this final section on "Specific Principles of Integrative Medicine Directly Related to You", we will discuss these forms of **natural energy production** and the how they can be used to **prevent** disease and help you maintain an optimal level of homeostasis (life-balance).

3c. Natural Energy Production & Utilization

One of Integrative Medicine's most important functions is to help you build an awareness of your 2-part nervous system (or control center). Seventy percent (70%) of your nervous system is considered to be **involuntary**, which means that the operations and functions it controls happen automatically without your consent or control. The remaining thirty percent (30%) is considered your **voluntary** nervous system and consists of **natural forms of energy production** that you consciously control. If used correctly, these natural forms of energy produced by your voluntary nervous system can be utilized to help bring balance and healing to your involuntary nervous system.

This is important because most of the time it is the **over activity of your involuntary nervous system** which causes imbalance, discomfort, or dis-ease to manifest in your life. The ability to access and harmonize your involuntary nervous system by utilizing **the natural forms of energy** produced through your voluntary nervous system is crucial if you want to maintain your overall health and well-being. Let's take a closer look at both parts of your nervous system so you can have a clear understanding of each part and the functions they are responsible for governing.

Your **INVOLUNTARY** Nervous system:

Your involuntary nervous system automatically operates most of the vital organs and systems within your body. For example, you do not have to command your kidney, liver, or heart to function, these organs function involuntarily and are controlled by your brain which is the command center for your entire nervous system.

Your involuntary nervous system is responsible for operating the major systems within your body like your circulatory system, digestive system, and immune system (just to name a few). These systems are absolutely vital functions of your body that you obviously do not control or operate. How you voluntarily decide to move, think, and feel with your body, mind, and emotions can effect these systems but their overall operation and function is controlled by your involuntary nervous system.

Your involuntary nervous system is also responsible for activating your "flight or fight" response. As stated in the previous chapter, this is a natural defense mechanism of your body's nervous system that is activated when you perceive yourself to be in a harmful or life-threatening situation. It causes many physiological changes that prepares your body to either run from perceived danger or fight to stay alive. The constant activation of your "fight or flight" response, especially when it is unnecessary can begin to weaken the systems and organs that your involuntary nervous system operates.

As you begin to realize how much responsibility your involuntary nervous system has it becomes clear how important it is to ensure that it maintains an optimal level of strength and stability. A strong involuntary nervous system means that your organs and the major systems of your body are healthy and in good condition. Now let's take a look at your voluntary nervous system and the three forms of natural energy it produces which can be used to directly access and influence your involuntary nervous system and help it maintain its balance and harmony. YOUR health and harmony!

Your **VOLUNTARY** Nervous System:

This part of your nervous system consists of...

-All voluntary **THOUGHT** signals you control and the **energy** they produce,

-All voluntary **BREATHING** rhythms you control and the **energy** they produce, &

-All voluntary **MOVEMENT** (or **ACTIONS**) you make and the **energy** they produce.

These are the three forms of **natural energy production** that you can control and utilize to access, influence, and heal your involuntary nervous system. As stated in the second chapter, "energy follows every thought that you have", so if you control your thought you can control where your energy goes. Mind-body exercise is fantastic because it guides you to focus your thought **first** on what is considered the most powerful form of natural energy, your BREATH!

In the previous chapter we discussed how your breath can be used to activate your "relaxation response" in order to counter or reverse the effects of the "fight or flight" response. It is very important to reiterate this fact because it is a great example of how your breath (a natural form of energy production) can be used (through breathing exercises/meditations) to bring balance and harmony to your involuntary nervous system. As it stated in the last chapter:

"Your breath is a natural tranquilizer for your mind and body, as soon as you focus your attention on your breathing and begin to control its rhythm it automatically triggers your voluntary nervous system to activate your relaxation response! This is why Breathing exercises are one of the most effective methods to use in order to reverse the onset and effects of stress, it works almost immediately! Your breath can be used in this way because it is both a part of your voluntary and involuntary nervous systems. This means that you can voluntarily make yourself breathe when you want to (like when performing breathing exercises), and your body also involuntarily breathes on its own (like when sleeping). Your breath is the bridge or connection that links the voluntary and involuntary parts of your nervous system together."

This example shows the power of your breath and how controlling its rhythm can bring immediate balance and harmony to your entire being. If you focus your thought on your breath and begin to produce relaxing rhythms of breathing they will eventually be translated into your involuntary nervous system and calm its over- activity. Your breath gives you direct access to your involuntary nervous system because it is a part of both your voluntary and involuntary nervous systems. It is a form of your **natural energy production** that if harnessed and utilized can begin to change and transform you into a more healthy, disciplined, and positive individual.

We will end this chapter on Integrative Medicine by taking a more in-depth look at two different forms of Mind-body Exercise. If any one of these exercises are practiced on a regular basis they can help you find the root cause of pain or discomfort in your life and at the same time guide you to an optimal level of well-being. These exercises are good for your complete being because they require you to use all three parts of your voluntary nervous system (your voluntary thought, breath, and movement) at the same time.

4. Mind-Body Exercise – Self-medication!

Mind-body exercise is referred to as self-medication because it guides and instructs you on how to use the **natural forms of energy** produced by your voluntary nervous system to access and heal your involuntary nervous system. It is basically using the powers within self, to medicate self! Even if you are not suffering from a disease or illness it is still intelligent to practice some form of Mind-body exercise, any repetition that strengthens your involuntary nervous system is also strengthening the organs and major systems it governs and controls. The practice of Mind-body exercise is also beneficial because it enhances your minds ability to perform mental transmutation by strengthening its ability to focus and concentrate.

4a. Mind-Body Exercise
<u>The Ultimate Power of your BREATH!</u>

The first and most important principle of mind-body exercise is to build an **awareness** and **appreciation** of your <u>breath</u>! You breathe approximately 23,000 times per day, and each one of these breaths represent a powerful fact - **you are alive**! These breaths also represent a natural form of energy which can be used to strengthen your entire being, so the question you must ask yourself is, "how many of these breaths do I control, utilize, or most importantly, appreciate?" Developing a knowledge and understanding of how powerful the act of breathing is will help you build a deeper appreciation for life and a higher level of self-awareness and self-respect.

At the beginning of most Mind-body exercises an individual is given a simple (yet powerful) breathing exercise that naturally relaxes their body and gives their mind a single point of focus (their **breath**). This automatically activates their "relaxation response" and puts the individual in the proper mood and mode to perform certain mind-body exercises which require focus and concentration like *Guided Imagery*. The only way to access the mind and begin to control your thought is by first relaxing the body, and the most natural and effective method of calming the body is by focusing on your breath.

Your breath is the master key when it comes to attaining an optimal level of health, and the best way to get acquainted with it is through breathing exercises and meditations (Breath-work). Before we discuss these mind-body exercises in more specific detail let's look at some amazing facts about your breath that if reflected on can improve your level of self-motivation and self-inspiration...

-In most modern and ancient cultures, the **breath** is considered as the "breath of life". This distinction is based upon the fact that without the action of breathing there is no living, no moving, no being, no life!
-The human body can live without solid food for months, without water for days, but it can only go without the oxygen provided through the process of **breathing** for minutes before permanent brain damage can occur and eventually loss of life.

-You **breathe** while you are sleeping! This is not just an amazing fact it is a constant miracle!

-The first thing we do once we leave our mother's womb is BREATHE! (In order for a newborn to cry it first must be breathing).

-Most forms of Integrative Medicine such as Acupuncture, Yoga, Qi-Gong, Guided Imagery, Progressive Muscle Relaxation, and Breathing Meditations all utilize the power of the breath in their methods.

-There are numerous medically proven benefits from practicing breathing exercises such as increased lung capacity, more oxygenated blood supply to brain and body, enhanced internal organ function, a reduction of stress and anxiety levels, improved energy levels, and improved sleep patterns (just to name a few).

4b. Breathing Meditations (Exercises) & Guided Imagery

The information provided below includes important tips and guidelines to keep in mind and follow as you begin to practice these **breathing exercises**:

(Instructions)

-Holding your thought on one thing is not the easiest thing to do, as you begin these exercises you might find that you have temporarily lost your focus and your mind has begun to wonder and think of other thoughts or images. If this occurs, **do not discourage yourself, encourage yourself**, simply accept the fact that you have temporarily lost your focus and slowly bring your attention and awareness back to your breathing and continue the exercise.

-When practicing the formal Breathing exercises that require you to be seated, find a comfortable chair and make sure your spine and lower back are supported. Laying on a bed or a flat cushioned surface is also an option. Try to find times during the day when you know that you will not be interrupted, distracted, or disturbed and make it a priority to do the formal breathing exercises at those times.

-Some breathing exercises are informal and do not require you to be seated, laying, or alone, they can be used at any time to activate your relaxation response, reverse the onset of stress, or calm a hectic situation.

-As stated before, **breathing exercises are most efficient when they are practiced daily**, even if it is only 2 or 3 minutes per day. This is how you reap the maximum benefits from these exercises, by performing them on a regular basis! This can easily be done because the informal breathing exercises provided can be performed while you are going about your daily activities, they do not require you to be stationary or take up a lot of your time.

-If you are just beginning to practice these breath-work exercises it is highly recommended that you **start slowly so your body can become accustomed to them**. This means that you do not need to make your breathing too deep or too slow as you begin these exercises, it is more important to get acquainted with the rhythm of breathing first before you try and make it deeper or slow it down.

Breathing Exercise #1 – Deeper, Quieter, and Slower

A sample of this exercise was provided in Chapter 3 to provide an example of how to activate your "relaxation response". Below I have provided the same exercise with more complete instructions, guidelines, and tips to follow. This is an informal Breath-work exercise and can be used at any time or in any place.

Directions:

Step 1: Pick a focal point (a place to focus on your breath). There are a two main points on your body that can be used to help you maintain a constant focus on your breath. These two focus-points include:

-**Your nose** (as you feel the air going in and out through your nostrils), &

-**Your chest** (as you feel it rising and falling with every inhale and exhale)

It does not matter which one you decide to use, there is no wrong or right choice, utilize the one that is the most comfortable for you or practice using both. These focal points are directly related to the action of breathing which means they can be used to help keep your focus and attention on your breath.

Step 2: Begin by focusing your attention on your focal point (nose or chest) and following the rhythm of your breathing for a few breath cycles. (If your focal point is your nose then focus your attention on the air traveling in and out of your nostrils, if it is your chest then focus your attention on the rise and fall of your chest as you inhale and exhale). After following your breath for a few cycles gently begin to control its rhythm by making it slightly deeper, quieter, and slower with each breath. Once you have reached a comfortable depth, speed, and rhythm of breathing you no longer need to make it any deeper, quieter, or slower, just maintain the rhythm you have created.

This is a gradual process, DO NOT TRY TO MAKE YOUR BREATH AS DEEP OR SLOW AS POSSIBLE ALL AT ONCE! The change in depth and speed of your breath should be very gradual, try to make each breath only 1% - 2% deeper, quieter, and slower as the one before it. Nothing about this breathing exercise should be uncomfortable, there should be absolutely no straining in this entire process. As mentioned previously, sometimes your mind can start to wonder and begin thinking of images and things other than your breath. If this occurs DO NOT DISCOURAGE YOURSELF, simply accept the fact that your mind has wondered, gently bring your attention and awareness back to your focal point, and continue to make your breath deeper, quieter, and slower.

Breathing Exercise #2 – Following Your Breath

This is another informal Breath-work exercise that can be used anywhere or at any time. It is considered one of the simplest breathing exercises to perform because it requires no action or controlled movement, just your focus and attention.

Directions:

Step #1: Pick a focal point (your nose or chest) and begin focusing on your breathing **without trying to influence it**. Do not try to speed it up, slow it down, or change its rhythm at all, just follow it with your mind and try to maintain your focus on it. As you focus on your breath without influencing it try and see if you can observe where the inhale begins or the exhale ends. The more you practice this exercise the easier it will become for you to observe your body breathing by itself! Just as it does when you are sleeping.

Tips:

As you attempt to follow your breath you may find that your attention wanders. Every time this happens gently bring your attention back to your breath by refocusing on your focal point, this will help you reestablish your focus and concentration so can continue to follow your breath. This is an informal breathing exercise and can be used at any time, especially in difficult situations. For example, if you find yourself in a stressful situation and can't seem to find a solution, focus your attention on your breath and begin to follow its rhythm. This direct focus on your breathing will immediately calm you down and balance out your emotions so eventually the solution can present itself. (Every problem is only a solution waiting to be found! You just have to be in the right state of mind to find it!) Also, if you have trouble sleeping due to over-thinking or restlessness try putting your attention on your breath and following its rhythm, this will help reduce your thoughts and calm your mind to the point where your body can more easily slip into the sleeping state.

Breathing Exercise #3 – Optimal Breathing

This is a formal breathing exercise that combines **abdominal breathing** and **chest cavity breathing** into one **Optimal Breath**. Once you start to practice this breathing exercise it will begin to increase your lung capacity, this in turn provides more oxygenated blood to your heart and enhances its level of function and capability!

Directions:

(This exercise is performed in three steps)

Step #1: Abdominal Breathing

Sit or lay in a comfortable position, if you are seated make sure that your back is supported and your spine is comfortably straight (if possible, ensure that your elbows are resting so you do not have to hold your arms in place). Place your hands palms down on your stomach and as you inhale slowly push your belly button outward and allow your stomach to expand until your lungs are comfortably full. You will feel your hands rise as you inhale. As you exhale, slowly push as much air out as possible by pulling your bully button in toward your spine. You will feel your hands begin to lower as you exhale. Do this for 5 – 10 breath cycles.

Tips:

GET THE RHYTHM DOWN FIRST, THEN WORK ON MAKING IT DEEPER AND SLOWER. It is ok if your breathing cycles are only 2, 3, or 4 seconds per inhale and exhale, they will naturally get longer as you gain more experience with the exercise. It is important to get the rhythm of the exercise down first, then work on making it deeper and slower. The focal point for this breathing exercise is your **abdomen (stomach/belly)**. If you lose focus and your mind begins to wander, bring your attention back to gently pushing out your belly as you inhale and gently pulling it in toward your spine as you exhale. This will automatically help you find your breathing again so you can continue to control its rhythm.

Step 2: Chest Cavity Breathing

Move your hands from your abdomen and place them palms down on your chest (either directly on your breasts/pectorals, or slightly above them on your upper chest, they key is to feel your chest rise and fall as you breathe! Also try to ensure that your elbows are resting so you do not have to hold your hands in place). As you inhale allow your chest to expand and rise until your lungs are comfortably full and you can feel the breath at the top of your throat. As you exhale, feel your chest begin to lower as you slowly push out as much air possible utilizing the intercostal muscles located between your ribs. Do not flex these muscles; simply feel them as they help to push all the air out of your lungs. Do this for 5 – 10 breath cycles.

Tips:

GET THE RHYTHM DOWN FIRST, THEN WORK ON MAKING IT DEEPER AND SLOWER. It is ok if your breath cycles are only 2, 3, or 4 seconds per inhale and exhale, they will naturally get longer as you gain more experience with the exercise. It is important to get the rhythm of the exercise down first, then work on making it deeper and slower. The focal point for this breathing exercise is your **chest cavity (rib cage)**. If you lose focus and your mind begins to wander, gently bring your attention back to your chest and allow it to expand and rise with each inhale and slowly lower and relax as you exhale. This will automatically help you find your breathing again so you can continue to control its rhythm.

Step 3: Optimal Breathing

Now we are going to combine the two previous breathing exercises into one **Optimal Breath**! (Remember! Get the rhythm down first, then work on making it deeper and slower)

Make sure you are still in the same seated or laying position that you were in for Steps 1 and 2. Place one of your hands on your stomach as you would when doing abdominal breathing and place your other hand on your chest as you would when doing chest cavity breathing. Begin by gently inhaling and allowing your stomach to expand and rise, as you exhale slowly push as much air out as possible by pulling your bully button in toward your spine. (Now begins the Optimal Breath). Start your next inhale by gently taking a full abdominal breath (feel your hand rise as your stomach expands), once your abdomen has fully expanded **with the same inhale** continue to breathe into your chest feeling your other hand rise as your chest expands and your lungs are comfortably filled with air. (The inhale is complete when you can feel the air at the top of your throat) To exhale just reverse the process. Exhale first from the chest cavity allowing your chest to sink slowly (feel your hand begin to lower), once all air has been exhaled from the chest **with the same exhale** push the remaining air out by exhaling abdominally pulling your belly in towards your spine until all air is out. This complete inhale and exhale cycle is considered an **Optimal Breath**.

Tips:

Once again, the rhythm of Optimal Breathing goes as follows: Inhale into your stomach (once full), continue the same inhale into your chest (until full). Then, exhale from the chest (once empty), continue the same exhale from your stomach pulling your belly toward your spine until all air is out. With practice and experience you will eventually be able to go directly into performing the **Optimal Breath** without having to do the other exercises first. Until then, perform at least 5 breath cycles of abdominal breathing followed by 5 breath cycles of chest cavity breathing before you begin practicing Optimal breathing.

4b. Guided Imagery

Guided Imagery is another **mind-body exercise** that can be used to activate your "**relaxation response**"! Your voluntary thought (focused thought) is a form of natural energy production like your voluntary breathing is, it also can be used to self-medicate and harmonize your mind, body, and emotions. Guided Imagery is a method of relaxation that focuses your mind on positive images in order to reduce or reverse the symptoms of mental anxiety and emotional distress. If used on a regular basis it can become very effective when dealing with certain mental imbalances that have a negative influence on your overall health like P.T.S.D., chronic stress, or depression.

Guided Imagery involves creating **positive thoughts (images)** in your mind that you can see, hear, smell, taste, and feel. This method is effective because your mind interprets these sensory images that you voluntarily create and makes the body perceive them as if they were real. This is how you activate your *relaxation response* utilizing imagery, **by creating and holding a positive image within**

your mind and experiencing it with your senses. These positive images can then be used as a form of self-medication to help you regain mental balance and find your positivity whenever your mind relapses and begins to relive negative or traumatic events from your past. Keep in mind that **energy follows every image you create in your mind**, it does not matter if they are negative or positive in nature. This means that even if you hold your thought on a negative experience from your past, the energy that follows will continue to enliven the (PAST) experience and keep it PRESENT in your life.

A good example of a mental health condition that can be treated using Guided Imagery is *Post Traumatic Stress Disorder*. This disorder is caused or triggered by either experiencing or witnessing a life-threatening event like warfare (combat), a natural disaster, a traffic accident, or anything else that might shock or scare someone. When you first witness or experience a traumatic event like this it usually triggers your "fight or flight" (stress) response, this reaction of your nervous system is normal when experiencing these types of trauma for the first time. It becomes dangerous for your health when your stress response is triggered **every time** you simply **think** of the same traumatic event, especially if it occurred in your past. This constant and unnecessary activation of your stress response when it is not life-threatening can eventually cause internal damage to your physical body. Guided Imagery exercises like "**finding a place of comfort and healing**" can be specifically utilized to reduce and eventually stop the unnecessary triggering of your stress response caused by P.T.S.D. It provides you with a positive image which YOU have created that diverts your attention away from the post-traumatic event and focuses it on **YOUR** place of comfort and healing.

In this section we have provided two Guided Imagery exercises that require no assistance from a practitioner. Just make sure that you read the directions first until you understand the process, then perform the exercise. Guided Imagery is a form of self-medication that is self-applied, once you become accustomed to it through repetition you can use it anywhere.

Guided Imagery Exercise #1: "Eating a lemon"
This guided imagery exercise is not intended to be a consistent exercise in your daily life. It is only intended to be practiced once or twice so you can have a better awareness of your mind-body connection, it clearly demonstrates how your imagination can cause real physiological changes to your body.

(Directions)
Step #1:
Close your eyes, take a deep breath, and relax. Imagine that you have a bright yellow lemon in your hands. As you see it in your mind consider the color and feel of it. Picture yourself holding a knife and cutting the lemon into quarters. Now bring a slice of freshly cut lemon near you lips and sink your teeth in it. Feel and taste the lemon's sour juice and pulp flowing through your mouth...

Chances are, simply imagining that you are eating the lemon will make you start to salivate! In a non-official survey of over 100 people, approximately 8 out of every 10 began to salivate when performing this imagery exercise. Your mind to body connection is amazing, a simple thought can cause physical changes to your body! The same way stressful thoughts can cause your body to trigger your stress response, positive thoughts and images can cause your body to activate its relaxation response! The following Guided Imagery exercises take you through the process of creating a place of positivity and comfort that you can always use as a focal point to redirect your thoughts and energy away from negativity or traumatic events from your past.

Guided Imagery Exercise #2:
"Creating a place of comfort and healing"

When first beginning this exercise find a place where you can sit or lay down comfortably without being interrupted or disturbed. Once you have performed this exercise numerous times and have become comfortable with your "place of comfort and healing" you can begin to use it anywhere.

There are two different variations of this Guided Imagery exercise, you can either create a "place of comfort and healing" on your own, or this "place of comfort and healing" can be a favorite place from your past. It does not matter which one you choose, the only requirement is that it is a place of harmony that makes you feel happy, comfortable, safe, and at ease. If you cannot think of a place from your past where you felt like this then create one!

(Directions)

Variation #1: "Choosing a place from your past"

Whether you are seated or laying begin by closing your eyes and taking a few deep breaths. If you have chosen a place from your past as your "place of comfort and healing", then now is the time to focus your thought on this location and picture yourself there. Utilize your senses to make the place real as possible, call to mind what it felt like to be there, the familiar sounds, smells, tastes, or images that felt good to you and made you feel comfortable. Try to make this image bright and clear in your mind as if you were physically there right now. Hold onto the positive feelings and images that this special place makes you feel, allow them to create a sense of comfort and healing that will eventually activate your relaxation response and place your body in total relaxation!

Keep this imagery as long as you can, if you feel your mind wandering to other thoughts and images do not discourage yourself. Simply bring your focus back to the place from your past that you have chosen as a place of comfort and continue to enjoy the imagery you are creating!

Variation #2:
"Creating your own place of comfort and healing"

Whether you are seated or laying begin by taking a few deep breaths. If you are creating a new place of comfort and healing, then now is the time to picture yourself in that location. Some examples of a place you might create could include a beautiful beach, a forest, a tropical island, or a cabin in the mountains (everybody has different preferences on what they might consider a place of comfort and healing, it is completely up to you).

Once you have chosen your destination begin by utilizing your senses to see, hear, smell, taste, and feel this new place of comfort and healing. For example, if you chose a beach, picture yourself laying down in the warm sand, feel the heat of the sun as it gently warms your body. Listen to the rush of the waves, taste the salt in the air from the ocean, and dig your fingers into the sand as you lay there. After feeling the sun take a quick dip in the ocean and feel the water cooling and refreshing your body. You can do whatever you want in your place of comfort and healing, as long as it is positive in nature and induces a good feeling. Instead of laying in the sand you might imagine yourself walking down the beach and taking in all the sights, sounds, smells, and feelings of your surroundings. The key is to utilize your senses as much as possible to make the imagery as real as possible. Your body will not know the difference and eventually the comfort and peace produced by imagining (holding your thought on) the special place will automatically activate your relaxation response.

For both variations, if you find that your mind has wondered and begun to think of other things do not be discouraged, simply bring your focus back to your "special place" and rediscover it with your senses. Every time that your mind wonders and you refocus your thought on your place of comfort and healing it strengthens your level of concentration and self-control! With practice you will eventually be able to maintain a constant focus on your place of comfort and healing without mental disruption. This capability will allow you to utilize your special place to combat negative mental states, control your emotional reactions, and maintain an optimal state of well-being.

<u>Tips:</u>

Some forms of chronic mental and emotional stress can produce symptoms such as flashbacks, nightmares, severe anxiety, or uncontrollable thoughts about what might have caused the stress in the first place. When these symptoms occur or begin to overwhelm you, simply focus your attention and senses on your place of comfort and healing, this will help divert your thought and energy away from the negative experience and channel it into a more positive place. If possible, try to practice one of these variations of Guided Imagery exercises at least once per day. Start with 5 minutes, as it gets easier you can double the time spent on Imagery and reap twice the benefits! The more you use this form of imagery the easier it will be to combat post-traumatic events in your life and redirect your energy into a better place.

There are also other essential keys to dealing with traumatic experiences from your past, they include:

- Learning to forgive, even if you cannot forget.

- Finding the "teaching point" behind the experience.

- There is no time machine so learn from the past, live in the present, & plan your future!

- Have more gratitude, do not take life for granted.

4c Meditational Fitness

Meditational Fitness provides a format with guidelines that help you maintain a constant awareness of your thought, breath, and movement while working out or performing a fitness activity. Just like with Breathing Meditations or Guided Imagery it requires you to utilize all parts of your voluntary nervous system (thought, breath, and movement) in unison. It does this by positively forcing you to control your breathing, form, and movement throughout your entire work-out, even during the rest breaks or cardio portions. You can add the Meditational Fitness format to any work-out or exercise and it will help you maintain self-awareness throughout the process and also help you reach your goals in a more expedited and efficient manner.

To add the Meditational Fitness format to your work-out simply follow the guidelines provided below:

#1 - Control your BREATHING!

-**Breathe per repetition!** (for example, if you are doing push-ups, exhale as you push your body up and inhale as you lower your body back down). Most exercises require a 2-part movement (unless it is a non-movement exercise like a plank), find a breathing rhythm that you can use for every exercise you perform during your work-out. There should be one complete breath cycle (inhale and exhale) per 2-part repetition. More examples include: Pull-ups (exhale as you pull your body up and inhale as you lower it back down). Squats (inhale as you lower your hips into the squat position and exhale as you raise your hips back to a standing position).

Find a breathing rhythm for every exercise and utilize it during every repetition!

-**Perform "recovery breaths" between each set of exercises!** If you want to provide as much oxygen to the heart as possible, then focus on your breathing and control its rhythm during your rest periods that come in between each set. A "**recovery breath**" is combination of a deep inhale (preferably through your nose, mouth is also ok), followed by an open-throat exhale (as if you were trying to fog-up a mirror so you could write something on it with your finger). Try a few recovery breaths right now... (deep and quick inhale, then open-up the back of your throat and exhale quickly like you want to fog-up a mirror, once again, deep and quick inhale, then open-up the back of your throat and exhale quickly like you want to fog-up a mirror). These are the same recovery breaths that athletes use, they are no different than the recovery breaths that a basketball player takes at the free-throw line before he shoots, or the recovery breaths that a football player is taking in the huddle before the next play.

When you begin adding recovery breaths to your rest periods start with no less than 10 - 12 between each set. After a few weeks you will notice that during your rest periods you are recovering faster than you did before. This means that your overall endurance has increased, and you no longer need to take 10 - 12 recovery breaths between each set before performing your next exercise. When this happens begin taking only 7 - 9 recovery breaths between each set. Go no lower than 7 recovery breaths between sets until you have practiced controlling your rest periods for at least 6 - 9 months and are comfortable with performing recovery breaths.

-**Find a breathing rhythm for your cardio exercises!** If you breathe per repetition when you are doing muscular endurance exercises like squats, push-ups, or pull-ups, then you should also find a rhythm of breathing when performing cardiovascular exercises like jogging, rowing, or biking. Once you find a breathing rhythm that matches the cardiovascular exercise, try to keep your focus and attention on it throughout the exercise. For example, a good breathing rhythm used when rowing is to exhale through the rowing motion (as you push and extend with your legs and pull with your arms), and inhale as you are preparing to row again. This steady rhythm of breathing ensures that your heart receives a constant and regular supply of oxygen while it works at an elevated level, it does this by matching your breathing with the stroking motion.

There are also other breathing rhythms that can be used for more popular forms of cardiovascular exercises like walking, jogging, or running. One of the most effective and commonly known breathing rhythms is referred to as "**Mindful walking/jogging**", it requires you to take a continuous 2-step inhale and a 2-step exhale as you walk or jog. This is one of the most popular breathing rhythms used by triathletes, marathon runners, and cross-country athletes because it ensures that your heart receives a constant and regular flow of oxygen as it works at an elevated rate.

If you want to try "**Mindful walking/jogging**" follow the instructions and tips provided below:

Instructions:

-Pick either your left or right foot and use it as a point of focus. This is the foot you will use to maintain your breathing rhythm; your inhale and exhale will always start as this foot touches the ground. If you lose your rhythm, simply look down or feel this foot touch the ground and you will find your rhythm again. <u>For these instructions we will use your left foot as the point of focus</u>. Begin walking (make sure that the pace is slightly faster than your normal walk), as you feel your left foot touch the ground begin your **inhale** and continue it as your right foot touches the ground (that was 1 inhale for two steps). Now you are back to your left foot, this time **exhale** as the left touches the ground and continue the same exhale as the right touches (that was also 1 exhale for two steps). Use the chart below to help you understand the rhythm even better!

Steps:	Left	Right	Left	Right	Left	Right	Left	Right
Breathing:	in	in	out	out	in	in	out	out

Tips:

-There are two recommended methods of breathing as you begin Meditational walking or jogging; either by breathing in and out of your mouth or breathing in through your nose and out through your mouth. Try both and see which is the most comfortable for you.

-To get the rhythm down first do it as you are walking. After you have the rhythm down you can speed it up to a slow jog and eventually use it to go as fast as you want. To move from a walk to a jog simply speed up your breaths so you can continue to match your steps. It is logical that you will begin to breathe a little faster as you begin to move a little faster.

-When first beginning this breathing rhythm do it for no more than 3-5 minute increments at a time until your body is comfortable with it and you can stay on the rhythm with ease.

-A small percentage of people who try this breathing rhythm for the first time may become slightly light-headed, if this occurs stop and take at least a 2-minute break before trying the rhythm again. As with anything, it may take your body time to adjust to this type of repetition, especially if you have never tried a breathing rhythm like this before.

#2 - Control your MOVEMENT!

-**Focus on your form**! Research your exercises, find the proper form for every exercise you are performing during your work-outs. This will ensure that you stay as injury-free as possible. BE AWARE OF YOUR SPINE AT ALL TIMES! With the majority of exercises your spine (vertebrae / back) should be straight. (AS MENTIONED EARLIER, DO NOT FORGET TO BREATHE PER REPETITION!)

-**Compound movements are the best!** Instead of working one muscle group per repetition, try compound exercises that work more than one muscle group per repetition. Examples include: squats with a shoulder press, lunges with biceps curl, or push-ups with a single-arm row. These types of compound exercises will help maximize your time, make

90

each set within your work-out more efficient, and ensure that you reach your goals in more timely manner.

Chapter 6:
My Goals, My Aims, My Objectives!

This chapter is intended to ensure that you have set personal and professional goals in your life that you want to attain in your immediate and long-term future. If you have a goal in your life and you want to reach it, you must put forth the necessary effort and energy needed to attain it. If you have no goals in your life then now is the time to ask yourself, **"What am I putting my daily effort and energy into?"**

Setting personal and professional goals enables you to shape your own destiny! It gives you a sense of purpose in your life. It sets you on a journey of personal success and achievement through self-determination and self-motivation. Most of the time to reach a set goal it requires sacrificing some of your "personal" or "free" time to accomplish the necessary tasks needed, and this requires a certain level self-control and self-discipline. These innate characteristics, along with patience and perseverance help develop individual WILL-POWER, and it is the cultivation and growth of your individual will-power that helps you reach your goals and maintain an optimal well-being.

As stated earlier, setting personal goals increases your will-power, and a lack of them diminishes it. **Do you have personal goals, aims, or objectives that you want to accomplish in your life? Are you putting forth the necessary effort and energy to attain them?** If not, then make a new contract with yourself! Utilizing the template provided below, write down your personal and professional goals and the values that you think are needed to reach them on a separate piece of paper. After filling in the required information, print and sign your name. **In signing your name, you will have created a contract between YOURSELF and the GOALS you would like to achieve.**

To keep your goals in mind, add a daily reminder to your phone, or take a picture of your goal contract and set it as your screen saver. Make copies of your contract to place around your house, they will act as a constant reminder of the promises you have made to yourself and provide some motivation to help get them done!

(Goal Contract Template)

Personal Goals: Professional Goals:
(next 1-12months)   (next 1-12 months)

_____

_____

_____

_____

Long-term: Long-term:
(1-5 years)   (1-5 years)

_____

_____

_____

_____

Personal Values & Characteristics: (needed to succeed)

_____

MY GOALS CONTRACT:

"I will put forth my best effort and energy to reach the professional and personal goals I have set for myself."

Print:_____

Sign:_____

Date:_____

Chapter 7:
Wellness Tips for an Optimal Well-being

Without leaving your home or buying anything there are very practical things you can do daily which will over time help you attain a more healthy and balanced well-being. Most people have a lot of responsibility in relation to their family, job, or friends, and sometimes this makes them forget that **they are (you, the individual)** one of the most important components in the entire equation! Meaning that if they do not take care of themselves, then how could they responsibly take care of someone else. Following some of the wellness tips provided in this chapter will help you find the balance, relaxation, and energy needed so you can fulfill your responsibilities to the best of your ability and at the same time take care of you!

CREATING A "PERSONAL SPACE" IN YOUR HOME...

Creating a personal space is simply finding a place within your home to work or relax that you can call your own and where you won't be disturbed. To create the right atmosphere within your personal space you can put objects that are significant to you and help you feel positive, peaceful, and progressive. Examples of things you can place within your personal space can include: a photograph of someone or something that invokes positive feelings and thoughts, a candle, some flowers or plants, a copy of your "relaxation list", a copy of your goal contract, your books or journal, whatever you like as long as it is positive in nature! It is important to have a place within your home in which you can relax and find comfort, a place where you can focus and concentrate on whatever you decide to put your mind and energy into.

YOUR "RELAXATION LIST"

Making a relaxation list (and using it) is a good way to help you maintain a healthy balance between work and relaxation. Sometimes you can be so focused on taking care of everything else you can forget to take care of yourself! Creating a relaxation list is a good reminder that you also must take care of YOU, and that means planning things into your daily, weekly, and monthly schedule that provide you with comfort and relaxation!

A copy of your relaxation list should be placed somewhere within the "personal space" you have created in your home. You should also place a copy on your refrigerator door, bathroom mirror, on your office desk at work, and even by your bed. Just having this list is no good unless you plan some of these things into your schedule and actually do them! Making an effort to find some comfort in your life helps you maintain the balance between work and relaxation, which is another essential part in maintaining physical, mental, and emotional balance and well-being.

An example of a "Relaxation List" might include activities such as:

-Taking a long shower or bath

-Going on a walk

-Playing music you enjoy, and more importantly – DANCING! (Even if you are alone)

-Reading a book in your personal space

-Talking with friends and family

-Swimming

-Getting a massage or spa treatment

-Enjoying a sunset or sunrise

-Practicing a breathing exercise in your personal space

-Practicing a guided imagery exercise in your personal space

-Spending time with someone who makes you feel good

-Volunteering (Coaching, Tutoring, Mentoring) Yes! Some people find it personally refreshing and invigorating when they help others. Helping produces happiness!

Creating your relaxation list should be an enjoyable experience, especially once you begin to use it! Use your list when you are bored and feel as though there is nothing to do. Use it when you feel things or situations in your life are becoming too heavy or intense and you need something to help you relax and calm down.

FINDING A NON-ELECTRONIC HOBBY...

Yes, it is the age of technology, but this does not mean your electronic gadgets have to be part of your entire day. You should intentionally set time aside and find activities and hobbies that are not electronic in nature. Anything from trying a new sport to learning how to sew will help you better yourself as a person. This is not only important for you but also for your friends, family, co-workers, and community. Electronic gadgets can become just as addictive as drugs, in some instances they can lead you to disregard other important obligations in your life resulting in some sort of pain or discomfort. Set a good example by turning off the TV, computer, video games, and even your phone every now and then, you will thank yourself in the future.

READ!!!

If possible, set 30 to 60 minutes aside in the evening (or whenever you can) for at least three days per week to read! Make a list of subjects you are interested in, go to a Bookstore (or on-line) and buy a few books that stimulate your interest. Any type of reading material is better than nothing to read at all! This is a perfect time to utilize the "personal space" you have created within your home, try to choose a time where you won't be disturbed so your full attention can be given to whatever you have chosen to read. Taking this time to read can become a positive habit that helps you find some much needed rest and repose from your everyday life, especially if you have found a subject or two that you enjoy.

FAMILY TIME

Spending quality time with your family should of course be a high priority in your life. Sometimes due to work obligations or the fact that both parents work it is hard to get the quantity of time we would like with our family. If this is the case, try to make sure that the time you do spend with your family is spent together and involves some sort of interaction and communication. Home is where the heart is, and if the family members living within the home are not in accord with one another it will usually lead to problems and issues that could have possibly been avoided if there was more communication! A great way to ensure open lines of communication with all members of the family is to try and have at least one meal together every day. Singles or individuals without immediate family members living with them should schedule outings and get-togethers with friends and make it a point to stay in consistent contact with their family, even if they are away from home.

VOLUNTEERING

In helping others, we also help ourselves! True happiness is the feeling you get when you have helped someone solve a problem, learn something new, or become a better person. Giving your time and energy to help someone is the best and most powerful gift that you can give. There are many organizations in every community that are always in need of some sort of assistance, guidance, or a helping hand. Without volunteers in most communities there would be no coaches, tutors, youth group leaders, or mentors to help guide and set the example for the younger generations to follow. **Learning how to sacrifice some of your free time for the benefit of others helps you <u>find</u> and begin to <u>feel</u> the non-material happiness that comes from within.** And REMEMBER, true volunteering is done without the hope of a reward or compensation, it is simply doing it because it is the right thing to do! Be an active and positive part of your community and VOLUNTEER!

Chapter 8:
Natural Nutrition

If you are what you eat, then **what have you been eating**!? Part of knowing self is understanding that what you consume eventually becomes you. The nutrients within the food you eat is the main source of energy used in producing the new cells your body needs to replace the old ones (this is **HOW** you are what you eat). Every system and organ in your body is composed of cells and operates mainly on a cellular level, and the overall health of these cells is determined by your diet, what **YOU** choose to eat! If you want the vital systems and organs within your body to function at an optimal level, then it is best to consume foods that are as close to their natural state as possible.

As "**Fact #13**" states in Chapter 2...

Your body and its many systems operate best when you consume <u>whole</u> foods full of vitamins, minerals, and other natural nutrients which <u>have not been altered, processed, or preserved</u>.

Why are nutrients that are natural the best for the body? Because your body, its many systems, and organs are completely <u>natural</u> functions, which means they require nutrients that are <u>natural</u> in their composition. What are some examples of things that are natural? It is natural for the seasons to change; it is natural for a bird to fly; it is natural for your kidney and liver to function; it is natural for your heart to beat and your cardiovascular system to operate.

These are all natural processes and actions that follow natural law. There is not a single component of your physical being, either internal or external, that is artificial, processed, or man-made. Your body functions as it is <u>naturally</u> intended to function, just like everything else in nature.

In chapter 2 we also discussed these two important facts...

What you eat determines how you move, feel, and age.
(Fact #11)

&

What you eat determines how your body fights disease.
(Fact #12)

If you want to know yourself more completely and understand why you move, feel, and age the way you do, then look at what you have been eating. If you have steadily gained weight over time and cannot seem to find out why, or if you have been at the same weight for a long time and cannot seem to lose anymore, **then chart what you are eating for at least two weeks and you will most likely find out why**. Weight loss is 70% diet (what you consume) and 30% activity (how much you move), most people think it is the other way around. This means that if you really want to lose weight it requires more self-discipline when it comes to your diet as opposed to just working-out. There are numerous apps that you can download today which help you track what you consume, but the best way to do it is with paper and pen because it personalizes the process and makes it more hands-on if you write it down.

Unfortunately, most Doctors will have you begin tracking what you eat <u>after</u> you have been diagnosed with an ailment like diabetes, obesity, or high blood pressure. **Why start tracking what you eat after you have developed a disease or imbalance?** If you track what you eat **now**, it could possibly help you prevent the onset of a disease by showing you exactly what your excesses and deficiencies are when it comes to what you consume. For example, in the process of tracking what you consume you might see that you are consuming an **EXCESS** amount of artificial or processed sugars which could possibly end up causing obesity or diabetes. Knowledge is power, and ignorance is dangerous! If you **know** and can see that you have been consuming too much sugar you can reduce this excess before it turns into a problem. Tracking what you consume and looking for the excesses and/or deficiencies is one of the best methods to ensure that you stay healthy and avoid unnecessary dis-eases and dis-orders. **The key is to balance out the excesses and deficiencies in your diet before they cause problems, but you can't do that until you know what they are!**

There is no healthy way to lose weight fast or change your complete diet in a week; these processes take time, education, personal effort, and consistency. Anything worthwhile is gained by taking small steps instead of giant leaps, this slow but **consistent** method ensures long-lasting success, even if it takes longer to get there.

The "ME" Diet program given in the next section of this chapter is a learning process that should be experienced at least once in your life. It sets you on a path of becoming your own nutritionist and cook, one step at a time. The knowledge you gain about "self" through this program in reference to what you consume, your imbalances (excesses/deficiencies), and how to correct them is invaluable and can definitely help guide you to better health.

THE "ME" DIET:

Throughout the next two to six weeks this "ME" Diet program will help you build a much better understanding of what you consume. This new knowledge will enable you to make the small but necessary changes to your diet needed to lower your risk of dis-ease and ensure your future health. Finding your imbalances is just one reason to track what you eat, there are also other important facts about "self" that can be learned from tracking what you consume.

Throughout this "ME" Diet program you will also learn...

...More about YOU! This method provides a complete overview of what you consume!

...What your **DAILY CALORIE BUDGET** is and what it has to do with your body weight.

...Facts about **SERVING SIZES** and **FOOD LABELS.**

...How to track what you consume using a "**Daily Food Intake Chart**"

...What **EXCESSES** and/or **DEFICIENCIES** are in your diet so you can work on equalizing them.

...How to make small but necessary changes to your diet that will ensure your future health.

...What type of "eater" you are? (emotional, excited, stressed, bored).

...How to structure and plan your meals and snacks.

Before you begin keep in mind that the entire purpose of this program is to eventually help you become your own personal nutritionist! You should not have to rely on someone else to plan or prepare your meals, or ensure that you are getting the proper nutrients, this is something that everyone should have the knowledge to do for themselves. Following this "Me" Diet program can help you start this learning process one step at a time.

Follow the steps given below to begin your own personalized "ME" Diet program. Steps 1 – 4 provide you with what you need to know before you begin, and the remaining steps provide you with specific directions on how to complete the program.

Step #1 - Find your <u>DAILY CALORIE BUDGET</u>...

This number will tell you how many calories you can consume daily to maintain your current body weight. The formula used to find this number takes into consideration your age, gender, height, weight, and level of physical activity. The average Daily Calorie Budget for women is between 1500 to 2000 calories per day, and the average for men is between 1700 to 2200 per day (it may be more depending on your level of activity). There are numerous "calorie calculators" on-line that can calculate your personal Daily Calorie Budget once you have entered the required information. Type "calorie calculator" or "how to determine my daily calorie budget" into an on-line search engine and find out what your daily calorie budget is **before you go any further with this program**. If you have no access to the internet you can find out your approximate Daily Calorie Budget by utilizing the formula provided in Appendix B.

Step #2 – Know your SERVING SIZES & FOOD LABELS

Before you begin tracking what you eat utilizing your Daily Food Intake Charts it is necessary to know and understand what "serving sizes" are so you can properly keep count of your calorie intake. Portions and serving sizes are two different things, a portion is how much you decide to eat for a meal or snack (portion sizes can be large or small, it depends on the individual), and a **SERVING SIZE** is a measured amount of food or drink, such as a **slice** of cheese, a **cup** (8 ounces) of juice, or a **tablespoon** of peanut butter. If you are going to track what you consume it is important to know the servings sizes of the foods you eat so you can properly chart your calorie consumption. This is where **Food Labels (Nutrition Facts)** come in handy, they break down the food in **serving sizes** and tell you how many servings there are in total, what the serving size is (1 slice, 1 cup, 1 tablespoon, etc.), and how many calories are within each serving. This information helps you know how many servings you ate so you can in turn calculate how many calories you consumed throughout the day. (See Appendix C)

Food labels or **Nutrition Fact labels** also provide other vital information such as how much fat, carbohydrates, or protein are in each serving, and what percentage of micronutrients (vitamins and minerals) are in each serving. This important information can help determine if you are getting the right amount of nutrients in what you eat! Always keep in mind that **your body has natural nutrient needs that must be provided through the food you eat!**

Knowing how to read food labels and understanding serving sizes is important as you begin to track what you consume. If you are going to follow this program you must at least know how to determine how many calories you are eating per serving. If you are at a restaurant or a friend's house and do not have a food label to reference, then familiarize yourself with the "serving size" chart provided in Appendix C. This chart will help you learn how to determine how many calories you are consuming no matter where you are eating. If you are truly eating on the run, just take a picture (of your meal/snack) and use it as a reference when it is time to fill out your Daily Food Intake Sheet.

Step #3 – Get acquainted with your <u>Daily Food Intake Sheet</u>
The Daily Food Intake Sheet provided in Appendix D (Diagram 1.1) is considered a good template to use if you want to track what you consume. Before you begin, copy the template provided in Diagram 1.1 on a piece of paper and make as many copies as you need. (You will need 1 Daily Food Intake Sheet per day for the entire program, so for example if you are doing the program for 2 weeks you will need 14 copies.

These are the sheets you will fill out at the end of each day. On the evening of the 7th day you will lay out all 7 sheets and evaluate them using the questions provided in step 5. This is the fantastic and eye-opening part of the program, seeing exactly what and how much you have consumed over the last week. Once again, BEFORE MAKING CHANGES TO

YOUR DIET YOU HAVE TO KNOW <u>WHAT</u> AND <u>HOW MUCH</u> YOU ARE EATING!

The questions you will answer when filling out your Daily Food Intake Sheet include:

-What foods/drinks did you consume throughout the day?

-How many servings of each did you consume?

-What time did you eat?

-What your level of hunger was at the time you ate?

-What your emotional state was at the time you ate?

The repetition of completing these daily food intake Sheets will help you build a new level of self-awareness in relation to what you eat, how much you eat, and the effect it has on your body. This is the information that you need to know before you can make any changes to your diet!

Step #4 – Pick a day to start!

Any day is a good day to start because this program is completed in weekly cycles, this means that if you started on a Sunday you would end your first cycle on Saturday. To get a good understanding of what you consume and the necessary changes that need to be made to your diet at least 2 weeks is recommended, no more than 4-6 weeks is necessary. Make **learning what you are, by tracking what you eat** a personal goal of yours (chapter 6), this will help provide you with the necessary will-power to follow through with the program.

Step #5 – GET STARTED!

To begin you will need:

-**Daily Food Intake Sheets** (utilize the template and diagrams from Appendix D)

-**A pen/pencil**

-**A food calorie list** that provides how many calories per serving.

(This is needed to determine your calorie consumption [per serving] of what you ate and your total calorie consumption for the day. Find an on-line search engine and type in "food calorie calculator" or "food calorie content per serving". There are numerous options, you can either download a food calorie list or use it on-line to determine your calories per serving. There are also apps you can download on your phone that provide the calorie content of foods per serving size).

Week 1:

During the first week of the program it is important **NOT** to make any changes to your diet, just eat as you have been so at the end of the first week you can evaluate your Daily Food Intake Sheets and see what imbalances (excesses/ deficiencies) you can find. Before making any changes you first must know what changes need to be made! **BE HONEST WITH YOURSELF**, only you will see these sheets, in order to balance out an excess or deficiency you first have to admit that you have it! This is easier to do once you see it on paper. Keep in mind that at the end of each week you will lay out your last 7 days of Daily Food Intake Sheets and evaluate them. If you are not honest with yourself while filling out these daily sheets it will make it more difficult to find your imbalances.

Days 1 – 6: (utilize the same process for days 1 – 6)

-At the end of each day, sometime after you have had your last meal/snack, take 10-15 minutes and fill out your Daily Food Intake Sheet (Columns 1-5). Fill out each column (what you ate/how many servings/the time you ate/your level of hunger at that time/ & your emotional state at the time). **Do not fill out columns 6 and 7 yet** ("calories per serving" and "total calories")! Fill out columns 1 – 5 completely before completing columns 6 and 7. (**see Diagram 1.1** – Appendix D) If you have issues remembering what you ate earlier in the day, how much you ate, the time you ate, what your level of hunger was, and what type of emotions you were feeling at the time, then take your daily food intake sheet with you and fill it out after each meal or snack. This way everything you ate is fresh in your mind, including how much you ate, your level of hunger, and what your emotional state was when you decided to eat. It takes no more than 30 to 60 seconds to fill out your sheet after each meal/snack. If you do not want to take your sheet with you then take a picture of each meal. You can refer to it later if needed to find out how many servings you consumed if you cannot remember how much you ate earlier.

-After completing columns 1-5, you can now answer the questions in the last two columns of the daily food intake sheet starting with column 6, "calories per serving". Utilizing a food calorie calculator (on-line or app), **find out how many** calories there are per serving for each food/drink item annotated on your sheet and write it down in column 6 (calories per serving). **(see diagram 1.1** – Appendix D) Once this column is complete you will have the information needed to fill out column 7 (total calories).

-Now calculate the total amount of calories you consumed per food item (column 7). This is done by simply multiplying the number in column 2 (number of servings consumed) with the number in column 6 (how many calories per serving). For example, if you ate 4 slices of bread, and each slice was 75 calories, your total calorie intake for the bread would be 300 calories. 4 slices x 75 calories per slice (serving) = 300 calories. **(see Diagram 1.1** – Appendix D)

-The last step is adding together all the numbers in column 7 (total calories), this number is your **total calorie consumption** for that day and should be written down under column 7 in the space titled "Total calories for the day". This number tells if you were above or below your Daily Calorie Budget for that day.

NOW YOU ARE READY TO EVALUATE YOUR LAST 7 DAYS

Day 7: (Evaluation)

-After you have filled out your Daily Food Intake Chart for the day, take your last seven sheets (including the one you just filled out) and lay them out in front of you.

-Starting with day 1, utilize the following questionnaire to check each day. If you find any excesses or deficiencies make a note of them on your sheet. **Keep in mind this is about you taking more self-responsibility for YOU!** Hopefully this

110

information can bring balance to any excesses or deficiencies before they lead to dis-comfort, pain, or disease.

(Questionnaire)

-How many cups of water did I drink?

-How many servings of vegetables did I eat?

-How many servings of fruit did I eat?

-How many servings of nuts and/or seeds did I eat?

-How many servings of whole grains/breads did I eat?

-How many servings of dairy products did I eat/drink?

-How many servings of meat products did I eat?

-How many servings of sweets (candies/chocolates) did I eat?

-What emotion did I experience the most when eating this day? Did it influence what or how much I ate? (if yes, use the guidelines given in chapter 4 on "how to track your emotions" so you can begin to track the emotion that causes you to eat even if you are not hungry. To break the habit of "emotional eating" you first must know what emotion is causing it!

-What was my level of hunger before consuming my meals/snacks this day? A healthy level of hunger is between 5 and 10. Or did I eat at times that I was not hungry (hunger level 1-4). Scale: 1 = not hungry, & 10 = very hungry

-What was my total calorie intake for the day?

-Was I above or below my Daily Calorie Budget? What foods put me over my daily budget?

-Did I eat/drink too much of something this day (excess)?

-Did I NOT eat/drink enough of something this day (deficiency)? (veggies/fruit/water/etc.)

-Now that you have gone through each day and have a better understanding of what and how much you consume, **choose 1 excess and 1 deficiency to stay aware of and change for the following week**. For example, you might have seen that over the last 7 days you did not drink enough water on some days, or you ate an excess of sweets or processed foods on some days. After you have chosen 1 excess and 1 deficiency make several notes of them and place them on your fridge, on your desk at work, write them on your next week's Daily food intake sheets, or add a daily reminder of them in your phone. **These reminders become affirmations of the changes you want to make to better yourself and your diet**!

-Read through the remaining **Diet & Nutrition Guidelines** provided in the next section. **Choose 1 or 2 guidelines/tips that you want to adopt in order to better structure your diet and ensure that you are getting the daily nutrients your body needs.** Add these guidelines/tips to your daily notes and affirmations as you did with the excesses and deficiencies you want to change.

WEEKS 2, 3, 4, 5, & 6

-For the remaining weeks of the program (which is up to you, at least 2 weeks is recommended), follow Steps 1 through 5 as you did in week 1. As you begin week 2, do not forget about the 1 excess and 1 deficiency you want to work on balancing out, and the 1 or 2 new guidelines you have chosen from the Diet and Nutrition Guidelines to adopt and use when deciding what to eat.

-end of instructions-

This "ME" Diet program is a personal journey that teaches **self-responsibility** when it comes to managing your diet. If what you eat determines the health of your new cells, and these cells are the building blocks of your body, then you might want to know and have some control over what you are eating! This program teaches you about YOU! What YOUR eating habits are, if YOU are getting the right amount of nutrients, if YOU are drinking enough water, if YOU have excesses or deficiencies in your diet that can become dangerous to your health. The information and knowledge gained about "self" throughout this process can help you avoid unnecessary pain, discomfort, and dis-ease if you heed the warnings and make the necessary changes. There are many illnesses that can be avoided merely by paying more attention to what you eat, keep in mind that eating is a voluntary action, you control it!

Diet & Nutrition Guidelines for an Optimal Health

Utilize the following **Guidelines** and **Tips** to help optimize your diet and make your decision-making process more intelligent and informed when it comes to what you consume.

Tips on HOW to STRUCTURE your diet:

-Always start AND end your day with 1-2 cups of WATER! If you have a problem with the taste (or non-taste) of water then infuse it! (See recipes in Appendix E)

-Eat Breakfast! Even if it is something small, preferably whole grains (bread, oatmeal) or fruit. This will activate your metabolism and provide your body/brain with good carbohydrates/energy to start your day!

-Make breakfast or lunch your largest meal, not dinner! Avoid too many carbs in the evening, this will allow your body to burn your second energy source – FAT! **DO YOUR OWN RESEARCH**! Use a search engine and type in "low or no carb meals". (See other options provided in the dinner portion of the Smoothie/Soup/Salad Diet)

-Reduce your addictive excesses one day at a time! For example, if you drink 5 sodas per day, try going to 4 sodas per day the following week, then 2-3 sodas per day the next week. Until eventually you have weened yourself from the soda addiction/habit. Find something to replace the soda consumption like infused water, or herbal teas that are naturally sweetened with stevia, raw honey, or agave nectar.

-Plan your meals and snacks in advance, and if you can, cook your own meals! Reduce trips to restaurants and more importantly to fast food restaurants. Take your lunch to work with you. Meals can always be prepared a day in advance, so there is no excuse!

-Plan and prepare your snacks in portion-sized containers to take to work with you. This will help you avoid unhealthy snack foods, maintain a healthier diet, and could also save you money.

-Eat a vegetable salad per day! Make sure that you use a combination of green leafy veggies like kale, lettuce, spinach, collard/mustard/turnip greens, along with other veggies like cucumber, broccoli, carrots, bell peppers, tomatoes etc. Use a variety of colors when it comes to the cruciferous (non-leafy) veggies, and make sure to vary your leafy greens from day to day or week to week. Make your own salad dressings! (See appendix E)

-Eat a fruit salad (a variety of fruits) per day! Fresh or frozen fruits are best. If you are diabetic choose fruits that have less sugar like apples, strawberries, cherries, blueberries, or raspberries and make sure that you keep an eye on your blood-sugar levels. A serving of fruit is a great snack idea!

-If it is difficult to have a vegetable and fruit salad per day, then have at least 1 leafy- green smoothie per day! It should be 3-parts green leafy veggies to 2-part fruit. This is almost like a multi-vitamin and will ensure that you get most of the necessary servings of veggies and fruits that you need per day. This leafy-green smoothie can be used as a meal instead of unhealthy and unnatural protein shakes or bars. You can have it as your breakfast, lunch, or dinner! Having at least one smoothie per day can also ensure that your body is receiving most of the nutrients (vitamins and minerals) it needs to stay healthy and function properly!

-Eat more soups! (Beans, lentils, peas, vegetable or mixed). Beans, lentils, and peas are great sources of important nutrients that the body needs. Soups can make you fill full without overdoing the number of calories you intake.

-Have a handful of nuts or seeds per day! The serving sizes and nutrient-value of nuts vary widely so make sure that you check the serving size and nutrient value of the nuts you choose to enjoy, this will ensure that you are not overdoing it. Unsalted and non-roasted (raw) nuts are the best, if they are salted then nuts with sea-salt are the best. When it comes to seeds, chia seeds or flax seeds are an excellent source of the omega 3 fatty acids your body needs. To add them to your diet you can drop 1 – 2 tablespoons in your smoothie, soup, or any sauce that you make for a meal.

-If you can, bake, broil, grill, or steam your foods (instead of frying). This will keep more of the nutrients in the food, even boiling your vegetables reduces the nutrient content.

-Drink more herbal teas (non-sweetened). If you want to sweeten it use raw honey, stevia, or agave nectar. Hot tea is a good way to curb your hunger in the evening if you are trying to reduce your carbohydrate intake.

-Use healthy oils to cook with and for salad dressings like extra virgin olive oil, coconut oil, avocado oil, flaxseed oil, or sunflower oil.

-Don't forget to use natural spices like Turmeric (add to your smoothie), garlic, ginger, cinnamon, saffron, oregano, cayenne pepper, rosemary, thyme, or sage. They provide important nutrients and can be added to most foods!

-Drink only 100% direct-pressed juices.

-Always check food labels! If there are more than 4-5 ingredients, think twice!

-To manage your portions better use smaller plates when eating.

-If possible, buy your groceries direct from the farmer or a "Farmers Market". Getting these foods direct from the source can decrease the chances of the food being processed, preserved, or full of toxins.

Foods to REDUCE and/or AVOID!

-Avoid processed foods, fast foods, dyed foods (food coloring), and artificially flavored foods!

-Reduce (or avoid) eating bleached foods such as white sugars, white flour, white pasta or white rice. Replace white sugar with natural sweeteners like honey, agave nectar, or stevia. Replace white flour with whole grain flours. Replace white rice and pasta with better sources of carbohydrates such as couscous, bulgur, or brown rice.

-Avoid foods with trans fats and polyunsaturated fats. DO NOT AVOID ALL FATS! Healthy fat choices include coconut oil, extra virgin olive oil, organic butter, flaxseed oil, and avocado oil (use these healthy fats for cooking and salads). Fats are just as essential as carbohydrates and proteins because they help your body absorb certain minerals and are also used as carriers for vitamins, A, D, E, and K. Healthy fats are also a source of energy for your cell membranes and many different hormones.

-Avoid meal-replacements such as store-bought protein shakes and bars. If you do want to replace a meal do it with a leafy green & fruit smoothie. Add chia seed, flax seed, spirulina, or green peas and it will become an even more complete meal replacement.

-Avoid table salt! Use sea salt or Himalayan salts.

-Avoid sodas, energy drinks, and artificially sweetened juices and teas. Replace with WATER, infused water, 100% direct-pressed juices, and fruit or herbal teas.

-Reduce alcoholic beverages, beer, and hard liquors. If necessary, replace with red wine.

-Reduce meat consumption (Or stop eating meat altogether). If you continue to eat meat, try eating more fish and lean meats like turkey or chicken. To ensure that you are getting enough protein you can also replace the meats with nuts, seeds, whole grains, beans, and peas which are all good sources of protein and fiber!

-Reduce dairy consumption in the form of cow's milk, cheese, cream cheese, sour cream, powdered milk, and sweetened yoghurts. Replace with other milks like coconut, rice, almond, or soy milk. Try healthier cheeses like swiss or feta.

DETOXIFY & CLEANSE!

The following "Detox" was created on the basis that - **"You are what you eat"**! It consists of a simple diet plan that is easy to follow and utilizes **ONLY...**

-Foods that are good sources of natural energy
(body & brain food),
-Foods that can be easily digested
(not altered, still in their natural state) &
Foods that are high in nutritional value
(full of vitamins and minerals–creates healthy cells!)

The purpose of a "Detox" is to detoxify and cleanse your body, especially your digestive system. Food and unused food particles that are not properly digested can begin to build up and leave harmful toxins and waste in your body. If this constant accumulation of toxins goes unchecked it can eventually lead to the weakening of your immune system, lower energy levels, and numerous other health problems that possibly could have been avoided. Fortunately, this build up can be prevented and reversed if you go through a process of detoxifying your body with natural food fibers that help clean out your digestive system and eliminate these dangerous toxins.

Your body is always seeking to be healthy and whole, whenever it detects harmful toxins it will utilize as much energy needed to try and rid itself of them. Your body gets this extra energy by redirecting it away from other vital systems and organs that need it. This lowers the ability of these systems and organs to work at an optimal level. The process of detoxing (or lowering the toxicity level in your body) helps direct this energy back into the other parts of your body that need it! As the toxic levels in your body begin to decrease, your energy levels, metabolism, and mental abilities like concentrating will naturally increase.

If you have never done a natural detox like this before then you should set your first goal to complete at least 1 day. Once you have gained the experience from successfully completed 1 day you can then extend it to 3, 5, 7, or 10 days! Logic and the law of cause & effect prove that the longer you follow this detox the better it will be for your body!

Your body can begin to accumulate toxins through many different food sources, so in this Detox you will **<u>avoid</u>** foods like...

-milk (butter, creams, cheeses),

-meat products (all),

-refined carbohydrates (white bread/rice/flour, pasta, pastries, breakfast cereals)

-alcohol (beer, wine, liquor),

-sweets (refined sugars, hard candy, chocolate bars)

-caffeine products (coffee, soda)

Natural Detox – Diet Plan

(1, 3, 5, 7, or 10 days)

PRE-BREAKFAST: (For all recipes see Appendix E)

1-2 cups	Room temperature water
1 cup	Lemon-water (optional)

BREAKFAST:

1 ½ - 2 ½ cups	Leafy green & Fruit Smoothie, **or**
2-3 servings	Fruit (ex. 2 apples & 1 cup of grapes or 1 banana & 2 cups pineapple)

MID-DAY SNACK: (1-2 cups of water! Not optional)

1-2 cups	Vegetable salad, **or**
1-2 handfuls	Nuts or seeds (ex. walnuts, sunflower seeds, cashews, pistachios)

LUNCH: (1-2 cups of water! Not optional)

1 ½ - 2 ½ cups	Leafy green & Fruit Smoothie, **or**
2-3 servings	Fruit (ex. 2 apples & 1 cup of grapes or 1 banana & 2 cups pineapple)

MID-AFTERNOON SNACK:

(Have the opposite of what you ate for the mid-day snack!)

1-2 cups	Vegetable salad, **or**
1-2 handfuls	Nuts or seeds (ex. Peanuts, sunflower seeds, cashews, pistachios, etc.)

DINNER: (1-2 cups of water! Not optional)

1 ½ - 2 ½ cups	Leafy green & Fruit Smoothie, **or**
2-3 servings	Fruit (ex. 2 apples & 1 cup of grapes or 1 banana & 2 cups pineapple)

AFTER-DINNER SNACK: (optional)

1 large cup of Herbal tea, 1 serving of fruit, 1 serving of veggies, or 1 handful of nuts/seeds.
1-2 cups of water before bed!

(Directions given on next page)
(Before trying this Detox make sure to consult your doctor first)

"DETOX" DIRECTIONS:

-For as long as you are on the Detox, consume **NO** dairy, meat, refined carbs, refined sugars, alcohol, caffeine products, or sweets.

-Make sure there is at least 1.5 hours in between each meal/snack.

-Drink water throughout the entire day! STAY HYDRATED!

-Do not skip any meals!

-A daily multi-vitamin is recommended during this Detox! Especially your B vitamins and Vitamin D!

-Have a minimum of 2 smoothies per day! Leafy greens are a very important part of the Detox (see the breakfast/lunch/dinner directions below)

-Prepare your smoothies in the morning, even if you are having one for dinner. (just put it in your refrigerator)

-Prepare your snacks in containers to take with you.

-If you have little to no experience with cleanses, start with 1 to 3 days, and then add to it!

-Reduce your physical activity by at least half while following this Detox and reduce the intensity of your work-outs by at least 1/3. When working out make sure to observe your heart-rate and take extra rest breaks when needed.

-Do not discourage yourself if you do not follow the detox 100%, this will only demotivate you. Instead you should give yourself credit for what you have accomplished and try to do better the next day! Small steps lead to BIG CHANGE! It takes 2- 3 weeks of consistency and regularity to form a habit, so get started!

Pre-breakfast: You should always start and end your day with water! Drink the 1-2 cups of room temperature water sometime within the first 10 minutes after waking up. Consume the lemon-water (see "Recipes") next, at least 30 minutes before you eat breakfast!

Breakfast/Lunch/Dinner: For this "Detox", breakfast, lunch, and dinner are the same. You do not need to have a smoothie for all three main meals, but make sure to have one for at least 2 out of the 3 main meals per day! (See Appendix E for smoothie recipes) Make sure the ratio from leafy greens to fruit is 3:2, this means 3-parts leafy greens to 2-parts fruit. The leafy greens will help clean your digestive system and expedite the toxin removal from your body! If you do not have a smoothie for one of these meals, then have the second option which is 2-3 servings of fruits (your choice). Make sure to vary your fruits and check the serving sizes.

Mid-Day & Mid-Afternoon Snacks: If you choose to have nuts and seeds as your first snack, then make sure to have the vegetable salad as your next snack. **During this Detox it is important to have at least 1 cup of vegetable salad daily! Utilize only tomatoes, cucumbers, bell peppers, or onions for your vegetable salads**! (see recipes in Appendix E) If you do not get a chance to have it for a mid-day or mid-afternoon snack, then have it in the evening as an after-dinner snack. Wait at least 1.5 hours after your last meal before eating your vegetable salad, and after you eat it, make sure to wait at least 1.5 hours before eating anything else.

After-Dinner Snacks:

-Infused water. (see "Recipes" – Appendix E) Also an option during the day.

-Hot Tea. Unsweetened herbal teas. **This is the #1 recommended after dinner "snack" (drink)!** Tea is also an option during the day. Try to have a minimum of 2-3 cups per day and make sure to vary your teas (chamomile, hibiscus, echinacea, etc.) only herbal teas! If these unsweetened herbal teas are difficult to drink you can add a teaspoon of raw honey or agave nectar to make them more enjoyable.

-A serving (1-2 cups) of veggies (ex. Sliced tomatoes & cucumbers or steamed/boiled broccoli/cauliflower/brussel sprouts, choose a cruciferous veggie). If necessary you can **lightly** season your veggies (only a dash) with natural seasonings like garlic, sea salt, ginger, rosemary, thyme, oregano, sage, pepper, or cayenne pepper (just to name a few). These are all-natural spices with great nutritional qualities and are easy to digest!

-A serving of stuffed olives with almonds or garlic pieces. In most large grocery stores they sale these types of stuffed olives fresh from their deli.

-A serving of fruit. (ex. a banana or apple)

-As stated earlier, if you forgot to have your vegetable salad for your mid-day or mid-afternoon snack, then have it as your after-dinner snack. **This meal should not be avoided!**

-If the snacks given above are not enough for you and the cravings are too hard to contain then try one of the following snacks: 2-3 dates/figs, or 1 sliced apple with a tablespoon of natural peanut butter, or 1-2 stalks of celery with a tablespoon of natural peanut butter.

Preparation!

-First you must know that this is NOT A DIET, it is a Detox. Even though you are temporarily changing your eating habits your body will still be receiving all the necessary nutrients it needs to heal and cleanse itself of toxins. If this is your first Detox then start with 1 day, if you decide to do it for longer be prepared for the first 3 days to be the hardest. Once you have made it past the initial 3 days your body will adjust and begin to adapt to the "Detox" meals as it continues to cleanse itself.

-Go shopping! Once you know how many days you are planning to follow the Detox it is smart to shop for everything that you need before you start. In Appendix E there are recipes for the vegetable salads and smoothies that can be used as shopping lists.

-end-

The Smoothie-Soup-Salad Diet!

Once you have completed your Detox it is important to try and find a diet that helps you reduce the amount of toxins consumed in the food you eat. This plan was put together utilizing the guidelines given earlier in this chapter entitled "Tips on how to structure your diet". It is specifically designed to ensure that you meet all your body's nutritional needs through the foods that you choose eat. Keep in mind that this diet plan can be altered or changed to fit your food personality. Your diet is what you choose to eat, so in time you must become your own nutritionist, dietician, and cook!

Pre-breakfast: (For all recipes see Appendix E)
1-2 cups of room temperature water
1 cup of lemon or grapefruit infused water

Breakfast: (1 cup of Hot tea or coffee with breakfast is optional)

Option #1	Option #2
2 slices whole-grain bread w/ peanut butter	1-2 cups of leafy green & fruit smoothie

Option #3	Option #4
1-1½ cups yoghurt w/ fresh fruits of your choice!	1-2 cups oatmeal w/ 1 tsp of raw honey

Mid-day Snack: (1-2 cups of WATER!)

Option #1	Option #2
1-1½ cups of nuts or seeds. Unroasted & unsalted is preferred Seas salt is ok	1-1½ cups vegetable salad. Cucumber, bell pepper, & tomato w/ home-made dressing

Option #3

1-1 ½ cups cottage cheese w/ chopped spring onions
(Avoid this option if you had yoghurt for breakfast)

Lunch: (1-2 cups of WATER!)

Option #1

1½ -2½ cups of soup. Bean, legume, lentil, vegetable, or mixed.

Option #2

2 cups of leafy green & fruit smoothie

Mid-afternoon Snack: (1-2 cups of WATER!)

Same as mid-day snack but pick a different option.
See extra snack options below.

Dinner: (1-2 cups of WATER!)

Option #1

2-3 cups of mixed leafy green salad with 2-3 types of other veggies (ex. spinach and romaine lettuce with carrots, tomatoes, and radishes). Use only home-made dressings!

Option #2

Any veggie & clean protein meal, some options include:

-Pineapple curry sauce with wheat noodles

-Cauliflower cream sauce with brown rice or couscous

-Bean, legume, lentil, or vegetable soup

-Egg omelet with veggies & cheese

-Spinach wrap with guacamole & sautéed veggies

-Black, pinto, and navy beans with brown rice & corn

-Whole wheat noodles with pesto and mushrooms

Option #3

2 cups leafy green & fruit smoothie

After-dinner Snacks:

(also for throughout the day if necessary)

1 large cup of Herbal tea, 1 serving of fruit, 1 serving of veggies, 1 handful of nuts/seeds.

(see Healthy Snacks List in Appendix E for other options)

DIET DIRECTIONS:

-Make sure there is at least 1.5 hours in between each meal/snack.

-Drink water throughout the entire day! STAY HYDRATED!

-Drink only direct-pressed fruit juices (in small portions, and not with meals)

-A daily multi-vitamin is recommended, especially your B Vitamins and Vitamin D!

-Drink 2-3 cups of herbal tea per day. (if necessary, sweeten with 1-2 tsp of agave nectar or raw honey)

-Have a minimum of 1 smoothie per day! For breakfast, lunch, dinner, or as a snack.

-Have a minimum of 1 vegetable salad per day.

-Prepare your smoothies in the morning, even if you are having one for dinner. (just put it in your refrigerator)

-Prepare your snacks (vegetable salads, nuts, or seeds) in containers to take with you.

-Maintain portion control, check your serving sizes.

-Do not skip the "pre-breakfast" or "breakfast options", if you are not hungry then a smoothie is the best thing to have for breakfast. This will help to cleanse your digestive system and get your metabolism going!

-Check the "food to avoid & reduce list" given earlier in this chapter on a weekly basis to ensure that you are avoiding foods that can be harmful to your health.

Pre-breakfast:

You should always start and end your day with water! Drink the 1-2 cups of room temperature water sometime within the first 10 minutes after waking up. Consume the lemon/grapefruit-water next, (see "Recipes" – Appendix E) at least 30 minutes before you eat breakfast!

Breakfast:

For option #1 you can add natural or unsweetened jam, organic butter, organic cream cheese, a slice of cheese, a slice of turkey or chicken, or sliced cucumbers and tomatoes to your whole grain bread. Other condiments for your bread not mentioned are also ok if they are natural and used only in small portions. For option #3 use fresh fruit if possible. For option #4 you can also use fresh fruits, raisins, chopped dates/figs, a tsp of agave nectar, a tsp of raw honey, or a tsp of cinnamon to sweeten your oatmeal.

Mid-day Snack:

For option #1 make sure to vary your nuts and check for serving sizes. For option #2 make sure to vary your veggies and use home-made dressings (see Appendix E). If you choose to have nuts and seeds as your first snack, then make sure to have the vegetable salad as your next snack (mid-afternoon or after-dinner snack). For option #3 you can also add fruit or a different veggie to your cottage cheese. The nuts, seeds and vegetable salads are the top recommended snacks to have at these times, but these are not the only options, see the "Healthy Snacks List" in Appendix E for more snack options.

Lunch:

This is where you start to become your own cook and nutritionist! Find a healthy/organic soup recipe and prepare enough soup for at least 2-3 days (this will be your lunch meal for the next few days). This is a great time to add beans, legumes, lentils, peas, and other important foods to your diet that are great sources of nutrition. If you do not have the soup, this can be the meal that you have your daily smoothie, the decision is yours!

Mid-afternoon Snack:

Same as mid-day snack but pick a different option. (See healthy snack options in Appendix E)

Dinner:

For option #1 make sure to vary your leafy greens and veggies daily, this is once again a time to learn how to cook for yourself and ensure that you are getting all the nutrients your body needs. You can also add other condiments to your salad like olives, feta, banana pepperoni's, jalapeno's, seeds (sunflower/pumpkin), or any other foods that are natural (in portion). USE HOME-MADE SALAD DRESSINGS, no store-bought dressings! For option #2 there are several options given that include clean proteins, healthy veggies, and natural carbohydrates that are light and easy to digest like quinoa, brown rice, or couscous. Pick a meal, do an on-line search to find a good recipe with the ingredients you have chosen, and start cooking! Try to use fresh or frozen foods, avoid canned foods and pre-prepared foods when cooking.

After-Dinner Snacks:

-Infused water. (see "Recipes" – Appendix E) Also an option during the day.

-Hot Tea. Unsweetened herbal teas. **This is the #1 recommended after dinner "snack" (drink)!** Tea is also an option during the day. Try to have a minimum of 2-3 cups per day and make sure to vary your teas (chamomile, hibiscus, echinacea, etc.) only herbal teas! If these unsweetened herbal teas are difficult to drink you can add a teaspoon of raw honey or agave nectar to make them more enjoyable.

-A serving (1-2 cups) of veggies (ex. Sliced tomatoes & cucumbers or steamed/boiled broccoli/cauliflower/brussels sprouts, choose a cruciferous veggie). If necessary you can **lightly** season your veggies with natural seasonings like garlic, sea salt, ginger, rosemary, thyme, oregano, sage, pepper, or cayenne pepper (just to name a few). These are all-natural spices with great nutritional qualities and are easy to digest!

-A serving of stuffed olives with almonds or garlic pieces. In most large grocery stores they sale these types of stuffed olives fresh from their deli.

-A serving of fruit. (ex. a banana or apple)

-As stated earlier, if you forgot to have your vegetable salad for your mid-day or mid-afternoon snack, then have it as your after-dinner snack. **This meal should not be avoided!**

-If the snacks given above are not enough for you and the cravings are too hard to contain then try one of the following snacks: 1 cup of stuffed olives (w/ garlic or almonds), 2-3 dates/figs, 1 sliced apple with a tbsp. of natural peanut butter, or 1-2 stalks of celery with a tbsp. of natural peanut butter. (see "Healthy Snack List" in Appendix E for more options)

-end-

This entire chapter has been dedicated to helping you take more self-responsibility for your own health by learning how to manage your diet intelligently.

-The **"ME Diet Program"** helps you find any unhealthy excesses or deficiencies.

-The **"Detox" Diet Plan** provides a natural way to cleanse your body of toxic build-up utilizing only natural, whole, and unaltered foods. &

-The **Smoothie/Soup/Salad** diet gives you a well-structured diet plan to use that provides all the nutrients your body needs and can be adjusted to fit your own personal food preferences.

You do not have to rely on a dietician or nutritionist, you can follow these guidelines and develop your own personal understanding of the foods you eat and how they affect your overall health. There is a thought before every movement you make, even the action of eating! This is something you control, therefore it is your SELF-Responsibility!

APPENDIX - A

The definition of

"SELF-RESPONSIBILITY"

FACT!

YOU, and only YOU, are responsible for the actions and decisionsthat YOU choose to make...

There are two distinct definitions of this word. The first is an overall definition and the second is a holistic definition of the word as it relates directly to you.

Self-Responsibility: (definition)

The state or fact of being responsible, answerable, or accountable for something within one's own power to control or manage.

Self-Responsibility: (holistic definition)

The ability to take personal control and responsibility of your own physical, mental, and emotional well-being by being mindful of how you decide to live, think, and feel.

Self-responsibility encompasses all words that begin with "self", such as...

Self-respect: Showing a genuine appreciation for LIFE by respecting the amazing body and mind you have been blessed with to journey through it.

Self-awareness: Knowing and understanding all components of self and the universal laws that govern your body, mind, and emotions.

<u>Self</u>-control: The ability to control how you decide to live, think, and feel you're your body, mind, and emotions.

<u>Self</u>-discipline: The ability to utilize your will-power for a desired purpose, goal, or level of well-being.

These "self" words and their meanings define aspects of your life that are within your power to manage and control, therefore by definition they are also your.........

##........**SELF-RESPONSIBILITIES!**

APPENDIX B

Determining Your *Approximate* – "**Daily Calorie Budget**"

The following formula is provided to help you find your "Daily Calorie Budget". This is the number of calories you must consume daily to maintain your current body-weight. There are several different "calorie calculators" on-line that can provide you with an accurate number for your Daily Calorie Budget once you have input your height, weight, gender, age, and level of activity. If you have no access to the internet utilize the formula provided below to find out *approximately* what your daily calorie budget is…

Take your body-weight in kilograms (ex. 80kg),

and multiply it by 23 (for females) or by 24 (for males),

example: 80kg x 24(for a male) = 1,920 calories per day (Daily Calorie Budget)

This individual would need to consume approximately 1,920 calories per day to maintain his current body-weight of 80 kilograms.

The above calculation of your Daily Calorie Budget does not include your level of physical activity. The more active you are the more freedom you will have in your diet, but the less active you are the more you have to watch your calorie intake. This is how weight-gain usually creeps up on you almost unnoticed, especially if you are not active. To understand how weight-gain/loss works you have to know that…

3500 calories = 1 pound

As an example, if you need 1,800 calories per day to maintain your current weight, but you eat an average of 2,000 calories per day, you will continually gain 1 pound every 17 days and not really notice it because it was a gradual weight gain and not all at once! The extra 200 calories eaten per day (not utilized as energy) eventually becomes added pounds to your body weight. All carbohydrates and proteins not used by the body are stored as fat by your body!

(+200 **EXTRA** calories per day **x** 17 days = 3,400 calories, almost 1 pound **gained**).

You can use this same equation to lose weight without adding any extra physical activity in your daily life. If you need the same 1,800 calories per day to maintain your current weight but eat only 1,600 per day, you will over time lose approximately 1 pound every 17 days. The same goes the other way around, if you subtract calories from your daily calorie budget on a regular basis you will eventually begin to lose weight. Since you are not supplying the body with the number of calories it needs daily to maintain its current weight through the food you eat it will begin to utilize your fat storage as energy, this equals weight-loss!

(-200 **LESS** calories per day **x** 17 days = 3400 calories, almost 1 pound **lost**).

Restricting your calories in an intelligent way and still ensuring your body gets good nutrients is one of the best ways to attain healthy and long-lasting weight loss. The same way you gain it should be the same way you lose it, body-weight that is lost gradually is sustainable weight-loss because it requires a certain level of discipline to successfully do it!

Avoid eating less than 1400 calories per day for a woman, & 1600 calories per day for a man.

Before trying a calorie-restrictive diet make sure to consult your doctor first!

Appendix C:

Food Labels & Serving Sizes

This is where **FOOD LABELS (Nutrition Facts)** come in handy, they break down the food in **serving sizes** and tell you how many servings there are in the total, what the serving size is (1 slice, 1 cup, 1 tablespoon, etc....), and how many calories are within each serving. This information helps you know how many servings you ate so you can in turn calculate how many calories you consumed.

(example food label – potato chips)

Nutrition Facts

about 8 servings per container   ← in total?

**Serving size 1 oz
(28 grams/about 13 chips)**   ← What the serving size is?

Amount per serving

Calories   150   ← Calories per serving?

How many servings

Servings Size Chart (hand & thumb references to serving sizes):

Hand Part(size)	Foods	Calories (approx.)
	Rice, Noodles	200
Fist, 1 cup	Vegetables	50
	Fruits	75
	Beef	160
Palm, 3 oz.	Chicken/Turkey	160
	Fish	150
1 Handful, 1oz.	Nuts (walnuts)	185
	Seeds (sunflower)	165
	Chia seeds/Flaxseeds	140/75
1 Thumb, 1 tbsp.	Peanut Butter	175
	Cheese/cream cheese	100/125
Thumb tip, 1 tsp.	Cooking/salad oil	40
	Raw honey/agave nectar	20

Recommended Daily Food Servings:

For a 2,000-calorie diet you will need the following amounts (approx.) from each food group.
These numbers may vary depending on your height, weight, age, gender & level of activity

Vegetables:
Eat 2½ - 3 cups per day

Fruits:
Eat 1½ - 2 cups per day

Whole Grains:
Eat 5 – 7 ounces per day

Nuts & Seeds:
1 – 2 cups per day

Dairy:
½ - 1 cup per day

Healthy Oils:
1-4 tsp per day

Appendix D

DAILY FOOD INTAKE CHART

*The following template/format can be used as the heading for your Daily Food Intake Charts.

Use the below diagram as a reference for

Diagrams 1.1, 1.2, 1.3, & 1.4

GOAL:_____   **(example)**   Water (cups):_____

Week:_____

Day:_____

(1)	(2)	(3)	(4)	(5)	(6)	(7)

Total Calories for the day:_____

Your Daily Calorie Budget is:_____

(+ / -):_____

Columns:

(When making your template place the below categories in their respective number slots on the Daily Food Intake Chart)

(1) Food consumed   (5) Present Emotion

(2) Calories per serving   (6) Total calories per item

(3) Time   (7) Total Calories

(4) Hunger Level (1 – 10)

Diagram 1.1 (Use the above diagram as a template)

Diagram 1.2 (Fill out columns 1 through 5)

Diagram 1.3 (Find out how many calories per serving)

Diagram 1.4 (Find out how many calories per serving)

Appendix E

-RECIPES-

Recipes for the Detox Diet Plan:

Lemon-water:

Thoroughly clean 1 lemon,
cut in half and remove seeds,
squeeze ½ lemon into 1 cup
of water and drink!
(you can use warm or cold water)

Lemon-infused Water:

Thoroughly clean 1 lemon,
cut entire lemon into slices, &
add them to 4 cups of filtered
or spring water. Refrigerate.

Vegetable Salad:

-Utilize only tomatoes, onions, cucumbers, or bell peppers for this salad.

-Have only 1½ - 2 cups of vegetable salad per meal/snack.

-Remember to wait at least 1.5 hours after your last meal before eating the vegetable salad. If you decide to eat it as your mid-morning snack, then make sure to wait at least 1.5 hours after eating breakfast before you eat the salad. If you decide to eat it as your mid-afternoon snack, make sure to wait at least 1.5 hours after you have eaten lunch before you eat the vegetable salad. AND, wait 1.5 hours after you have eaten the vegetable salad before you eat anything else. This will ensure that the salad is properly digested.

Directions:

-Pick a single veggie or a combination of veggies from above, cut them into bite-size pieces, and put them into a bowl.

-Add 1 - 1½ tbsp. of either extra virgin olive oil, avocado oil, or sesame oil.

(OPTIONAL) Add 1 – 2 tsp of a natural seasoning like sage, sea salt, dill, garlic, or cayenne pepper. (other options are available, just make sure that it is a natural herb or spice)

Leafy-Green Smoothies:

-Make sure to keep the ratio 3:2! (3 parts greens-2 parts fruit)

-Make sure to chew your smoothies, it will help to produce the saliva needed for proper digestion.

-Utilize a variety of leafy-greens (options given below) & fresh or frozen fruits (avoid canned fruits)

Directions: (using a blender)

-Add water & leafy greens to blender and blend thoroughly until there are no more large pieces of greens.

-Add fruits (your choice, abbreviated list given below). If you are diabetic choose more low-sugar fruits.

-Add 1-2 tbsp. of a natural protein (your choice), either spirulina, ground chia seeds, ground flaxseed, or ground hemp seed and blend again until thoroughly mixed.

-(OPTIONAL) Add other superfoods (given below) and blend again.

-For more liquid smoothies add additional water. If you do not use frozen fruits and you still want your smoothie cold, then add a ½ cup of ice when you add the fruit.

-(OPTIONAL) If necessary you can add 1 - 2 tbsp. of stevia as a natural sweetener. If you are craving something sweet or have problems with the taste of the smoothies this may help.

Leafy-green options:

(raw leafy greens are a fantastic source of natural nutrients!)

- Spinach
- Bok Choy
- Turnip Greens
- Collard Greens
- Dandelion Greens
- Rucola
- Kale
- Romaine Lettuce
- MustardGreens
- Beet Greens

(This is NOT all the options for leafy greens, to find more do a quick search on-line)

Fruits:

(If you are diabetic use fruits which are lower in sugar)

Pineapple, papaya, mango, peach, plum, pear, apricot, melon, oranges, banana, kiwi, grapes, figs, dates.

Fruits with lower amounts of natural sugar include: blueberries, cherries, strawberries, raspberries, lemon, lime, apples, cranberries, and grapefruit.

(This is NOT all the fruit options, to find more fruits do a quick on-line search)

Optional Superfood Additions:

(these "superfoods" are packed with nutrients the body needs)

- Turmeric
- Chlorella
- Tahini
- Reishi Mushrooms
- Ginger
- Rice Protein
- Maca Root
- Avocado
- Cinnamon
- Soy Protein
- Wheatgrass Juice
- Coconut Oil/milk
- Pea Protein
- Goji Berries
- Acai Berries

Smoothie Recipes:

There are hundreds of smoothie recipes available on-line today. Your job is to find the ones that fit your personal taste **AND** help to fulfill your body's natural nutrient needs! Below

I have added 3 smoothie recipes that can be used during the Detox to ensure you are getting the proper vitamins, minerals, anti-oxidants, and phytonutrients your body needs to function at an optimal level and cleanse itself in the process!(For each recipe follow the directions given above)

Each recipe provided will make **three** complete servings (36-42 ounces), it depends upon how much water is used. To make enough for only 2 smoothies divide the ingredients by one-third. To make enough for just 1 smoothie divide the ingredients by two-thirds.

Smoothie Recipe #1
-2 cups of water
-2 ¼ cups kale (3 handfuls)
-1 apple, cored
-1 cup pineapple
-1 cup strawberries
-3/4 cup blueberries
-1 tbsp. of spirulina
-1–2 tbsp. of stevia (optional)

Smoothie Recipe #2
-2 cups of water
-2 ¼ cups spinach
-2 bananas
-2 cups mango
-2 tbsp. ground flaxseeds
-1–2 tbsp. of stevia
(optional)

Smoothie Recipe #3
-2 cups of water
-1 ½ cups Kale (2 handfuls)
-1 ½ cups Spinach (2 handfuls)
-2 cups strawberries
-1 cup raspberries
-1 cup blueberries
-2 tbsp. ground chia seeds
-1–2 tbsp. stevia (optional)

Smoothie Recipe #4
(protein smoothie)
-1 ½ - 2 cups coconut water
-1-2 tbsp. natural nut butter
(peanut or cashew)
-1 banana
-2-3 tbsp oats
-1-2 tbsp. ground chia seeds

Recipes for the Smoothie/Soup/Salad Diet Plan:

Lemon-water:

Same as above with extra options: Add a 1 tsp. of agave nectar, raw honey or stevia per cup (optional)

Lemon-infused water:

Same as above with extra options: Add 1 tbsp. of agave nectar, raw honey, or stevia per 2 quarts of water (optional)

Fruit-infused water:

-Take 2 cups of your favorite fruit (frozen or fresh)

-Cut the fruit into small pieces and add to a large drinking pitcher, bottle, or container.

-Add 6-8 cups of water, for a stronger fruit taste use only 6 cups)

-Add 1-2 tbsp. of stevia or 1 tbsp. of agave nectar (optional), mix & refrigerate.

Soup Recipes:

Now is the time to become your own cook. For this meal a bean. Legume, lentil, or vegetable soup is recommended. A mixture of both (bean & veggie) would also be a good choice. Do an on-line search for (healthy, organic) soups that peek your interest and utilize only natural ingredients. Make enough soup to have for lunch over a 2-3 day period so you don't have to cook soup every day, this means you would have to make at least 6-8 cups. Keep this in mind when searching for soups and shopping for the ingredients. Provided below is a simple and healthy soup option.

Home-made Salad Dressings:

Provided below are a few home-made salad dressing recipes to use for your salads. Use these dressings for your dinner salads in the Smoothie/Soup/Salad diet plan. If you would prefer to use another salad dressing just make sure that it is home-made and only utilizes natural ingredients. There are plenty of natural or organic salad dressing options available on-line, pick 1 or 2 that sound good and try them!

Balsamic Vinaigrette & Oil
(makes 6 servings, 115 cal, per serving, 2 tbsp. = 1 serving)
Ingredients:
-1/3 cup organic balsamic vinegar
-2 tbsp. of sunflower oil
-1 tbsp. agave nectar
-¼ cup minced red onions
-½ tsp. garlic powder
-½ tsp. sea salt
-2-3 pinches of ground pepper (add more to taste)

Directions:
Mix ingredients together in a bowl. Cover and refrigerate after using. This dressing will last about 1 week, so make sure to prepare enough for only 2 - 3 servings. Shake or stir before serving.

Caesar Dressing
(makes 6 servings, 50 cal. per serving, 2 tbsp. = 1 serving)
Ingredients:
-1 cup non-fat plain Greek yogurt
-3 tbsp. lemon juice (freshly squeezed)
-1 tbsp. extra virgin olive oil

-1 tbsp. Dijon mustard

-1 tsp. ground garlic powder

-½ dried oregano (or powder)

-½ dried dill (or powder)

-½ tsp. sea salt

-½ tsp. ground pepper

Directions:

Combine ingredients together in a large salad bowl and whisk thoroughly until mixed, then refrigerate for at least 1-hour before serving. This dressing will last 1 week, so make sure to prepare enough for 2 – 3 servings. Shake or stir before serving.

Sweet Honey Mustard Dressing
(makes 6 servings, 35 cal. per serving, 2 tbsp. = 1 serving)
Ingredients:

-¾ cup non-fat plain Greek yogurt

-1 tbsp. Dijon mustard

-1 tbsp. yellow mustard

-1 tbsp. raw honey or agave nectar

Directions:

Mix ingredients together in a bowl. Cover and refrigerate after using. This dressing will last about 1 week, so make sure to prepare enough for only 2 – 3 servings. Stir before serving.

Condiments:

Provided below are a few great-tasting condiments which are easy to make at home and can be used to liven up your meals or snacks! These can be good replacements for mayonnaise, sweetened ketchups, sweetened barbeque sauces, store-bought dips, and other condiments with unnatural preservatives and additives.

Hummus (home-made!)

Ingredients:

-2, 15-ounce cans of chickpeas

-1 tsp garlic powder

-½ cup virgin olive oil,

-4 tbsp. fresh lemon juice

-4 tbsp. tahini (optional)

-1 tsp ground cumin

-1 ½ tsp. sea salt (or Himalayan salt)

-½ tsp ground paprika

Directions:

Add the chickpeas, garlic, olive oil, lemon juice, tahini, cumin, and salt to your food processor and puree (if you do not have a food processor, add to a large bowl and mash/mix (2-3 minutes) as if you were making mashed potatoes. Once it is thoroughly mixed, place the finished hummus in a serving container, sprinkle with 1 tsp. of olive oil and the ½ tsp. of paprika, cover and refrigerate.

Guacamole (home-made!)

Ingredients:

-3 Avocados

-1 ½ cups diced tomatoes

-½ cup minced red or white onions

-½ cup fresh cilantro (chopped)

-1 lemon, halved and remove seeds

-½ tsp of sea salt (or Himalayan salt)

-½ tsp of ground cayenne pepper

Directions:

Cut the avocados length-wise, twist open, and spoon-out the flesh into a large mixing bowl. Add the lemon halves by squeezing both into the bowl, use a fork and mash/mix the avocado and and lemon juice until it is the right consistency. Add the rest of the ingredients and mix/stir thoroughly until desired consistency. Place the finished guacamole in a serving container, cover tightly and refrigerate.

Salsa (home-made!)

Ingredients:

-2 cups diced tomatoes

-¼ cup chopped or minced red onions

-2–3 tbsp. of freshly chopped cilantro

-2–3 tsp jalapeno, minced (optional)

-1 garlic clove, minced

-½ squeezed lemon or 1–2 tsp lemon juice

-½ - 1 tsp of sea or Himalayan salt

Directions:

Add all ingredients into a large mixing bowl and mix thoroughly. If you want a salsa that is less chunky, add the ingredients to a food processor and puree until desired consistency. Place the finished salsa in a serving container, cover, and refrigerate.

Healthy Snacks List:

Most store-bought snacks are so processed and pumped full of artificial sugars, dyes, salts, and other non-natural ingredients that they have lost most of their nutritional value. Being a busy person is no excuse for not eating right, all you have to do is prepare! Pick a couple healthy snacks you like and bring them with you on your "busy" day. The following snack options can be used as healthy alternatives.

-Infused water (recipe provided)

-Stuffed olives with garlic, almonds, or feta cheese

-Cottage cheese with 1 tsp raw honey, or chopped spring onions, or fruit

-Raw veggies with home-made hummus

-Rucola with strawberry and watermelon

-Plain Greek yogurt with fruit (your choice)

-Apples with cheese (swiss, gouda, feta)

-Apples with natural peanut butter (1 tbsp. per apple)

-Celery with peanut butter (1 tbsp. per 2 celery stalks)

-Pitted cherries with almonds

-Non-sweetened Herbal teas (if necessary sweeten with 1-2 tsp of stevia, agave nectar, or raw honey)

-Dairy-free dark chocolate (at least 70% cocoa). No more than a 1 ounce serving, 3-4 times per week

-Veggie wraps, use home-made sauce!

-Quinoa or couscous salads

-Small servings of split pea or lentil soup

-Whole grain pancakes with unsweetened apple sauce

-Raw veggies with home-made guacamole

-Veggie chips (sweet potato, kale) with home-made salsa or guacamole

-Cucumbers slices with mozzarella or feta (add natural seasoning if necessary)

-2–3 figs or dates

-A hard-boiled egg with sliced tomatoes on whole grain toast (season as necessary)

Notes:

Made in the USA
Columbia, SC
10 December 2019

84625542R00090